pfs:® Software Made Easy

CARL TOWNSEND

Osborne **McGraw-Hill**
Berkeley, California

Published by
Osborne **McGraw-Hill**
2600 Tenth Street
Berkeley, California 94710
U.S.A.

For information on translations and book distributors outside of
the U.S.A., please write to Osborne **McGraw-Hill** at the above
address.

A list of trademarks appears on page 259.

pfs:® Software Made Easy

1234567890 DODO 8987654

ISBN 0-88134-147-9

Cynthia Hudson, Acquisitions Editor
Denise Penrose and Kevin Gleason, Technical Editors
David Kruglinski and Phil Fawcett, Technical Reviewers
Ted Gartner, Copy Editor
Deborah Wilson, Composition
Yashi Okita, Cover Design

Table of Contents

Introduction

PFS:®*SOFTWARE Made Easy* is a tutorial that takes you step by step through the process of using PFS programs. It is designed to help you become a proficient user of programs produced by Software Publishing. Concepts are introduced, explained, and illustrated by examples that are of particular relevance to businesspeople and professionals.

How to Use This Book

Like any tutorial, this book is not just to be read. As you go through its chapters you should be sitting at your computer keyboard, trying the commands and functions as they are described. This "hands-on" experience is the best way to learn and master the PFS programs.

This book is divided into three parts. Part One describes five PFS programs in detail: PFS:WRITE, a word processing program; PFS:FILE, an information-management program; PFS:REPORT, a tabular report generator; PFS:GRAPH, a graphics program; and PFS:ACCESS, a telecommunications program.

Part Two is focused entirely on the many uses of PFS:FILE. You will learn how to design files, how to locate information stored in them and to move that information to other files, and how to redesign files.

Part Three shows you how to increase the usefulness of PFS programs. A major feature of these programs is that they can be used together in various combinations, so Part Three will teach you how to use the programs as an integrated package. You will also learn how PFS programs can work with information that was generated by non-PFS programs. In addition, three programs from PFS:SOLUTIONS are described: MAIL LIST, TICKLER, and LEDGER.

Finally, there are seven appendixes. You can use some as convenient references. There is a compendium of useful terms; a table listing and defining the PFS commands; and detailed descriptions of the hardware requirements of each program. You can use the other appendixes to acquire additional information of various kinds: detailed instructions for "installing" the programs; a description of the equipment needed for using PFS:ACCESS; advice on naming files; and instructions for using PFS programs on the Apple and TI computers.

What You Will Need

The PFS programs described in this book will work on the IBM PC and PC XT computers, the Apple IIe, IIc, and III computers, and the TI Professional computer. For the programs to work on them, all of these machines must have at least 128K of memory, except the Apple IIe and IIc, which require 64K. (If you are unsure how much memory your machine has, consult your dealer.)

The discussions in this book assume you are using an IBM PC or PC XT. If you are using an Apple IIe, IIc, or III, or the TI, consult Appendix G to learn how to use the PFS programs on your machine.

To use the PFS programs you will need at least one disk drive—two are preferable—or a hard disk system. You will also need a monitor (monochrome or color) and a printer. Your operating system (the program that enables your machine to perform and to run your PFS programs) must be MS DOS or PC DOS.

In each chapter that introduces a PFS program, you will be reminded that the program should already be "installed" for your system. Installation is the process of setting up your PFS program for your specific monitor, disk drive, and printer. Often your dealer will have installed the program for your system at the time of purchase. If this is not the case, refer to Appendix C, which describes how to install each of the programs covered in the book.

PART
ONE

Mastering PFS Programs

CHAPTER
ONE

Getting Started
With PFS

We live in a world that is exploding with information. Each of us accesses and assimilates large amounts of information daily. This information can change almost as rapidly as we use it. Many futurists say we have moved into an *information age* or *communication age*. Our ability to access, use, and manage information can determine our success in this new age. The PFS family of software is a tool to help you use and control information.

PFS software products are simple but powerful programs for information management using a personal computer. Here are the five members of the PFS software family that are described in detail in this book:

- PFS:WRITE is an easy-to-use word processing program that still gives you some of the power of a dedicated word processor.

- PFS:FILE is an information management program with comprehensive filing, sorting, and searching capabilities.

1

- PFS:REPORT is a report generator program that can be used with the files created by PFS:FILE to summarize data, perform calculations, and report the data in a convenient form.

- PFS:GRAPH is a graphics program that draws presentation-quality bar, line, or pie charts from data created by PFS:FILE, Lotus 1-2-3, or VisiCalc files.

- PFS:ACCESS is a program for sending and receiving information from another computer system by telephone lines.

All of these programs are *integrated,* which means that information can be moved from one program to another. For example, a document created with PFS:WRITE can include reports compiled by PFS: REPORT and graphs generated by PFS:GRAPH. Integration enhances the usefulness of any piece of information: once it has been entered into a program, it never needs to be entered again, and it can be used in a variety of ways. Chapter 11 describes how all the PFS programs work together.

Another PFS software product, PFS:SOLUTIONS, is a collection of application packages that interface with the other PFS programs. PFS:SOLUTIONS includes the applications MAIL LIST, INVEN-TORY, and LEDGER. These programs are examined in Chapter 13.

APPLICATIONS FOR PFS SOFTWARE

Most of the information we use each day is dynamic—constantly changing. Such change makes proper information management all the more critical. For example, one computer vendor discovered that a client was using seven address files with many duplications among the files. When a customer's address changed, it was updated in some files but not in others. Anyone needing the customer's most recent address could not determine which address was correct. With PFS:FILE, all of those addresses could have been kept current in a single file.

This next example shows another type of problem PFS software is designed to avoid. If you are a typical businessperson, you will write many reports and perhaps duplicate material from one report to the next. Graphs and charts can help reinforce a conclusion but are time-consuming to create. Often the same data is used to create additional charts with only slight changes to keep them timely. PFS:GRAPH will eliminate the need to draw even the first graph or chart. All you need do is decide on the information to be charted and then see which type of chart best displays that information.

PFS:FILE helps locate specific information quickly. If you often are the speaker at meetings or luncheons, you might want to have a quotation file with quotations stored by keywords. Using PFS:FILE, you can quickly locate those quotations and print them in the draft of your speech, which you are creating with PFS:WRITE.

PFS software can improve productivity in almost any application involving the management of information. PFS software is easy to learn and use and easy to relearn as well if you only use the programs occasionally.

All of the PFS programs are menu-driven, so you do not have to remember *function* and *option* names to use the programs. The programs are all inexpensive and have excellent error recovery if things do not go as you expected.

You can use PFS:FILE with PFS:REPORT for many applications: financial applications include general ledger, accounts receivable, accounts payable, job costing, invoicing, payroll, and budgeting. Other business applications include mailing list management, tickler files, employee record maintenance, inventory control, purchase order systems, project management, time scheduling, and order entry systems. Home applications include checkbook balancing, mailing list management, budgeting, stock portfolio management, nutritional management, recipe files, budget analysis, and cataloging.

USING PFS SOFTWARE

Before you learn the individual PFS programs, there are procedures you will need to become familiar with because they apply to PFS in general.

The PFS Keyboard

PFS programs use the computer keyboard differently than other similar software products. (Figure 1-1 shows the IBM PC keyboard.) The ENTER (or carriage return) key has no special command properties. Instead, the F10 key is the important key. If you are used to programs

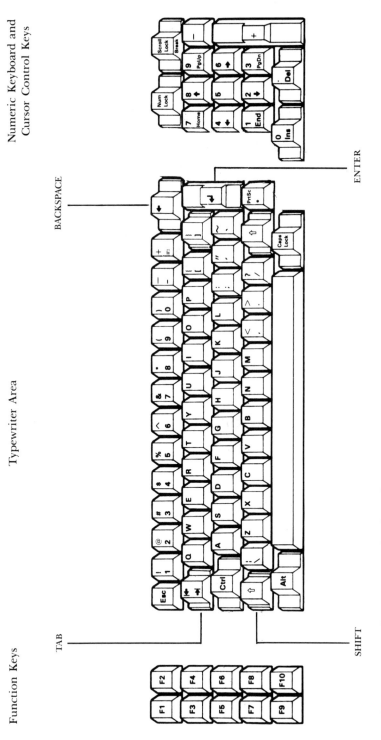

Figure 1-1. *The IBM PC keyboard*

made by other manufacturers, you may have some difficulty using the F10 key as the primary key in the PFS programs.

You move through the PFS program menus with the TAB key, and when you get where you are going, you press F10 to begin your task. The arrow keys and the PGUP, PGDN, and BACKSPACE keys work as you would expect them to work. The DEL key deletes the character the cursor is over, not the character to the left of the cursor as it does in some programs. Each repeated use of the DEL key deletes the character under the cursor and moves the next rightmost character to the left and under the cursor. Holding down the DEL key will continuously delete characters.

Disks and DOS

If you are running PFS on an IBM PC, you are also using either MS DOS or PC DOS as your operating system. PC DOS is designed specifically for the PC, and MS DOS is used on a wide variety of computers, including machines that are IBM-compatible. The different versions of MS DOS have various degrees of compatibility with PC DOS, so if you have an IBM-compatible system that uses some version of MS DOS, your system may or may not work with PFS programs. Check with your dealer or computer manufacturer to be sure.

If you are using PC DOS version 2.0 with floppy disk drives, you should be aware that some PFS programs are so large that you will not be able to install the operating system on the program disk. This is not a serious problem; however, it means that you start your computer with a DOS disk and then replace that disk with a PFS disk.

Although running PFS programs on a computer with a single disk drive is not impossible, some of the programs are more difficult to use this way. Not only will you have to do many disk swaps, but you will also have difficulty in backing up the data disks, since the sorting and copying functions in the PFS programs will not work with a single disk drive. (The backup procedure is described later in this chapter.)

Backing up your data disks is highly recommended, but backing up most of your PFS program disks is impossible if you have floppy disk drives. All PFS program disks but one *cannot* be copied. The one exception is PFS:ACCESS, of which you can make one copy. Some programs are sold with a copy of the program disk to give you a margin of safety. The programs can be installed on a hard disk by means of a special utility program.

After you have used the PFS programs a while, you are likely to have a great deal of data stored on many disks, even if you are using a hard disk system. As a rule, you should not mix data types on a single data disk (except, of course, on a hard disk). Mixing data types may seem harmless enough at first, but doing so will cause increasing inconvenience and confusion as you accumulate data. For example, if you are creating a mailing list, your file may start out small, and you may wish to put another file, such as a schedule of your appointments, on the disk with it. But the mailing list file will grow and you will eventually need the space occupied by the schedule. Removing it to another file will be a tedious process. Mixing a wide variety of types of information also makes it difficult to label a disk properly.

Be sure to use labels to identify your disks. These labels can be put on before or after the files are created on a disk. Once a label has been placed, be sure to use only a felt tip pen to add information—no pencils or ballpoint pens, which can damage the internal magnetic disk. Refer to Chapter 11 for further help with file management.

Naming Files

All PFS programs store information in *files* on disks. The PFS programs use part of DOS to create and manage these files. You use the DOS DIR command to see the names of the files on your floppy or hard disk. A detailed description of how this and other operating system commands work is beyond the scope of this book. Before you use PFS software, you should be familiar with the basic operating system commands like FORMAT, COPY, and DIR used to manage disks and files. Be sure you understand your operating system before doing the examples in this book. Read the manual that came with your system or consult any books available on it.

Each file stored on a disk has a name. Each file name on the disk must be unique and not used for any other file on that disk. This name is used to access or change the file. Each file name is made up of two parts, which are separated by a period: for instance,

MODEMS.BAK

The first part of the name can have as many as eight characters, which can be letters or numbers or both. It makes sense to give a file a name that indicates something about its contents. In the previous example, MODEMS indicates that the file contains information about modems. You should avoid special characters like "?", "<", or "[" in your file names because many of these characters are used by the operating system for other purposes. The operating system will automatically capitalize any lowercase letters you use in the name.

The second part of the name, called the *extension* and consisting of no more than three characters, generally indicates something about the *type* of file. For example, BAK indicates backup files. You can create your own extension conventions if you like (such as LTR for letters), but you should avoid using those that the system already uses for other purposes (such as COM, EXE, and BAS). Appendix F lists extension names that should not be used for PFS data files and lists suggested names.

You can name your files without giving them extensions. (The examples in your PFS program manuals do not use them.) However, extensions will give you better control over your files. For example, if you want to copy all files of a certain type and you have given them the same extension, you can copy them all with a single command. Using consistent extension names also helps you identify immediately the types of files stored on the disk (such as LTR for a letter file).

Disk Drive Designators

Whenever you want to store or retrieve a file, you should specify the disk drive where the file is to go or be found. That is, specify the drive with the data disk. For example, if your MODEMS.DAT file is on the data disk in Drive A, you can indicate this by using "A:" in front of "MODEMS.DAT":

A:MODEMS.DAT

If you do *not* specify any disk drive, the operating system will assume the drive for the data disk is the *same* as the program disk drive, which is correct only if you are using a hard disk or a system with a single disk drive. As a precaution, always use drive designators so you will always know *where* the information will be stored. In some cases you may write a file to the disk on one drive (say, B:MODEMS.DAT) and then read it from another drive (A:MODEMS.DAT). The designator is *not* a part of the file name, but only tells the operating system where to send or find the file.

Backup Procedures

Information stored on a disk has value—not only the value of the information itself, but also the monetary value of the time it took you to load the information to the disk. Often the loss of a file can mean the loss of many hours. On a typical IBM PC floppy disk, you can store a complete book manuscript. Imagine the time it would take to reenter this information if the disk were to become damaged.

Information can be lost in two ways. The most common cause is an operator error. For example, you might enter a document to PFS: WRITE and then leave the program without saving the document; or you might inadvertently erase an important file. (The ERASE command can erase an entire disk in seconds without so much as a cautionary note to the operator.) The second cause of information loss is a true hardware error or an error caused by an external environmental event. For example, a power surge could destroy a document you were creating with PFS:WRITE and had not yet stored on disk.

Because information can be easily lost or erased, save it periodically and back up your disks. Disks are cheap compared with your time. In creating documents with PFS:WRITE, take the time to stop and use the Save function to write the document to the disk periodically. (With PFS:FILE, the file is created on the disk as you enter the information.) Whatever PFS program you are using, after a work session (perhaps every four hours), back up the disk; that is, create a copy of any disk you have updated. Backing up the disk is a fundamental procedure of good management in any computer installation, regardless of the size of the computer.

With an IBM PC, back up your disks with the COPY command that is part of the operating system. Also verify any copies you make. *Verification* is the comparison of the copy with the original to be sure that no errors were created during copying. Verification can be done in any of three ways. One way is to use the "V" (for verify) option when you execute the COPY command. A second way is to use the VERIFY ON command before starting the copy or when first starting the system by putting the VERIFY ON command in the AUTOEXEC.BAT file (refer to your operating system manual for help). The third method to verify is to use DSKCOMP to check the new disk you have created. This third method is useful if you have used DSKCOPY, a program that can copy disks but that does not verify after copying. Be sure you use the right combination of COPY command and Verification option. With a hard disk, you can use the BACKUP command to create a backup of the hard disk. This, like DSKCOPY, does not verify the copy. For important files, use COPY. If you need more information on how to create your backups, refer to your DOS manual or a book on the DOS operating system.

CHAPTER
TWO

Using PFS:WRITE

Before you begin this chapter, be sure PFS:WRITE has been installed for your computer system. In most cases, the dealer who sells you PFS:WRITE will do this at no extra charge. If PFS:WRITE has not been installed, refer to Appendix C for instructions.

In addition, be sure you have enough computer memory to meet PFS:WRITE's requirements. A document is kept in the computer's memory as you create and edit the text. If you have more than 128K of memory, a document should contain about sixteen pages of text. If you use exactly 128K of memory, your documents will be limited to about fourteen pages each. Expanding your computer memory to 256K, however, will not permit you to edit a larger document. Sixteen pages is the maximum document size. If you were to write and edit a book using PFS:WRITE, you could never store more than one chapter as a single document, and this document could never exceed 32,000 characters.

WORD PROCESSING WITH PFS:WRITE

In this book, *word processing* refers specifically to the use of computers to create, edit, format, and print text. The words "word processing" were coined by IBM in 1964 to describe the Selectric typewriter, which used magnetic tapes. The primary goal of this early system was to reduce repetitive typing and to make correcting errors easier. PFS:WRITE has these same goals.

Word processing usually involves four processes:

- Creating and editing the document
- Formatting the document
- Saving the document
- Printing the document.

Beginning users often have trouble considering editing, formatting, and printing as three separate processes, since conventional typewriters format and print the text as it is entered. With PFS, *creating* and *editing* refer to entering and changing text. *Formatting* a document means arranging the text for printing by specifying the desired margins, page length, headers, and footers. *Saving* refers to keeping a document on disk for a future revision. *Printing* means creating the document on paper or other media.

With PFS:WRITE, the editor, formatter, and printer are all presented as separate menu items. Before beginning a document, you select the Define Page Menu from the Main Menu to set up the format of the document. The document is formatted on the screen as it is created or edited. If you want to change the format of the document later, say, set different margins, you only need to select the Define Page Menu again and define the new margin settings. The document is immediately reformatted. You then select the Get/Save/Remove function to save the document, and the Print function to print it.

The appearance of the printed document will be evident to you since the text image appears on the screen exactly as it will be printed. Margins and page breaks are shown, and the text is formatted. Any boldface will be shown on the screen in boldface. But PFS:WRITE also lacks many of the popular formatting features of more expensive programs: PFS:WRITE cannot justify both the right and left margins together, and center- and right-justification are only performed one line at a time.

```
PFS:WRITE MAIN MENU
-------------------


1  TYPE/EDIT        4  GET/SAVE/REMOVE

2  DEFINE PAGE      5  CLEAR

3  PRINT            6  EXIT



   SELECTION NUMBER:




F1-Help                                        F10-Continue
```

Figure 2-1.   *The PFS:WRITE Main Menu*

Since all of the PFS:WRITE functions are selected from a single Main Menu (see Figure 2-1), you do not need to remember function names. The menu is displayed when you start the program, and you initiate a specific function that will lead you to a choice of options.

Starting Up PFS:WRITE

Turn on your computer and select one of the following procedures for starting up (loading) PFS:WRITE:

Using an IBM PC with DOS 1.1 and a single floppy disk drive   Put the disk with PFS:WRITE (which includes an operating system) in the single drive and start the operating system (press CTRL, ALT, and DEL at the same time) from this drive. Enter the date (mm,dd,yy) and press ENTER. PFS:WRITE should then load and display the Main Menu.

Using an IBM PC with DOS 2.0 and a single floppy disk drive   Put the operating system disk in the single drive and start the system from this drive (Press CTRL, ALT, and DEL at the same time). Enter the date when requested (mm,dd,yy) and press ENTER. When you see the system prompt, remove the system disk and insert the PFS:WRITE program disk in the drive. Type in the following:

A>**WRITE** ENTER

Using an IBM PC with DOS 1.1 and two floppy disk drives The PFS:WRITE disk is normally installed with the operating system on the program disk. Insert this disk in Drive A and a blank, formatted disk in Drive B. Start the system (press CTRL, ALT, and DEL at the same time). Enter the date when requested (mm,dd,yy) and press ENTER. PFS:WRITE should load and then display the Main Menu.

Using an IBM PC with DOS 2.0 and two floppy disk drives In this case the operating system is too large to fit on the disk with the PFS:WRITE program. Start the system (press CTRL, ALT, and DEL at the same time) from a disk that contains the operating system using Drive A. Enter the date when requested (mm,dd,yy) and press ENTER. Then remove the disk with the operating system and put the disk with PFS:WRITE on Drive A and a blank, formatted disk on Drive B. Type in the following at the system prompt:

A>**WRITE** ENTER

Using an IBM PC with a hard disk or IBM PC XT In this system PFS:WRITE is normally installed on the hard disk. Start the system by pressing CTRL, ALT, and DEL at the same time, enter the date (mm,dd,yy), and press ENTER. To set the hard disk as the default drive, type **C:** after the prompt as shown:

C>**C:** ENTER

Then enter the program name:

C>**WRITE** ENTER

If you have a hard disk system, you will not need to change disks since the data will be stored on the hard disk. If you are using a system with two disk drives, put the data disk in Drive B. If you are using a system with a single disk drive, remove the PFS:WRITE program disk and put your data disk in Drive A. Your data disk should be a blank, formatted disk. The DOS manual explains how to format a disk. *Be sure the data disk has been formatted, or you will not be able to save your work or finish the procedures outlined in this chapter.*

SETTING UP FOR EDITING

Once PFS:WRITE has been loaded, the Main Menu (shown in Figure 2-1) is displayed. The cursor is next to the prompt for the "SELECTION NUMBER:". To begin the Type/Edit function, enter a 1 (Type/Edit) and press F10. (Remember, you do not use ENTER to enter a selection.) You will now see a screen that looks very much like a blank piece of paper (see Figure 2-2). Near the top left of the screen is a small, blinking line called the *cursor*. The cursor always marks the position where characters you type will be displayed and entered in the document. The cursor can be moved about the document using the CURSOR CONTROL keys on the right side of the keyboard (see Figure 1-1). The starting cursor position is six lines down from the top of the page and ten spaces over from the left margin.

The default page boundaries are marked on the *ruler line* for a standard 8 1/2 × 11 inch sheet of paper. As you enter text, the page is displayed as it will be printed, except that you only see 22 lines of the text. In effect, the screen is a window that permits you to see only a part of the document. The page shown in Figure 2-2 is empty because nothing has been written on it yet. At the bottom of the page, the ruler line shows the cursor position, margins, and current tab settings. The current margins are shown with brackets. Each tic mark on the ruler line represents one character position, and a bright rectangle indicates

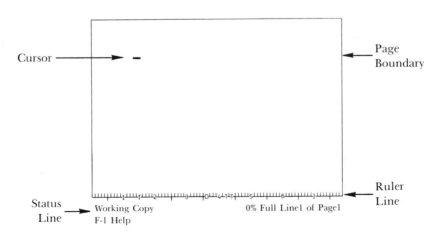

Figure 2-2. Preparing to enter the text

the cursor position. Below the ruler line is the *status line,* a line that reports the following information: whether the text is a working copy, what percent of space the text occupies in the computer's memory buffer, the line and the number of the page that is being edited. It also tells you how to get help.

Function 2 (Define Page) on the Main Menu is used to set margins and page length. To get to the Define Page Menu from the present screen, press ESC, enter **2** (Define Page), and press F10. You will see the display presented in Figure 2-3. You use the TAB key to move the cursor from one menu option to another. You can also use the SHIFT key with the TAB key to move the cursor back to a previous option. For now, leave the margins and page length at the default settings shown in Figure 2-3. Press F10 to return to your document, which is still a blank page. This entry procedure can be used on all menus: use the TAB key to move about the menu, choose any desired option, and then press F10 to continue. The TAB key is used to move the cursor forward in a screen; the SHIFT and TAB keys are used to move the cursor backward.

Press ESC to return to the Main Menu. Function 1 (the Type/Edit

```
                        DEFINE PAGE MENU




              LEFT MARGIN: 10      RIGHT MARGIN: 70

              TOP  MARGIN: 6       BOTTOM MARGIN: 6

              PAGE LENGTH: 66




     HEADING:

     FOOTING:



     F1-Help                                           F10-Continue
```

Figure 2-3. *Setting the margins and page length*

```
                              February 28, 1984


        Mr. John Smith
        22400 SE Milwaukie Way
        Portland, OR  97200

        Dear Mr. Smith:

             Thank you for your interest in the fares for our
        Willamette River Cruises.  The cruises run from June 5 to
        September 5.  Our 1984 fare schedule is as follows:

             Adult               $15.00    one-way
                                 $25.00    round-trip

             Children            $10.00    one-way
             (5-11)              $15.00    round-trip

             Child                         (no cost)
             (under 5)

             Senior Citizen      $12.00    one-way
                                 $21.00    round-trip

             Trips leave Portland daily at 8:00 a.m. and 1 p.m.  Each
        round-trip cruise lasts four hours.  Enclosed is a brochure
        with further information.  We look forward to having you sail
        with us.

                              Sincerely,


                              Adam Long
                              Sales Manager
        st
        Enclosure
```

Figure 2-4. *Sample letter*

selection) is used to enter and edit text. Enter **1** next to the prompt for "SELECTION NUMBER:" and press F10 to return to the editor. Again, the empty page will be displayed.

Before you can practice editing, you must have something to edit. Refer to the letter shown in Figure 2-4. First you'll see how to set the normal and decimal tabs this letter requires, and then you'll enter the document into the computer's memory using the keyboard.

You need several tab stops to enter the sample letter correctly. To set the tabs, press F2. Notice that the cursor is now on the ruler line. Use the CURSOR CONTROL keys to move the cursor either direction. Use the SPACE BAR to move the cursor to the right.

Tabs are set by typing "T" or "D." Normal tabs work the way typewriter tabs do and are set with T. Decimal tabs align decimal points in columns of numbers and are set with **D**. Leave the tab at 15 and set one additional normal tab at 42 (move the cursor to 42 and type **T** and a decimal tab at 36 (move the cursor to 36 and type a **D**). When you have set the tabs, press F10 to return to your document. Notice that the cursor has returned to its normal position on the screen.

Entering the Document

Your tabs are now set and you are ready to enter the sample letter. Use the tab at position 42 to enter the date at the beginning of the letter. Use the ENTER key to skip a few lines, and type the address and the greeting.

February 28, 1984

Mr. John Smith
22400 SW Milwaukie Way
Portland, OR 97200

Dear Mr. Smith:

   Thank you for your interest in the fares for our Willamette River Cruises. The cruises run from June 5 to September 5. Our 1984 fare schedule is as follows:

Don't worry about mistakes as you enter the letter. You will correct them later. Concentrate on developing a steady entry of text. You can use the BACKSPACE key to back up a few characters and retype if corrections can be made quickly, but this should be the limit of your editing while entering this text.

Do not press ENTER at the end of a line to return to the left margin except at the end of a paragraph. PFS:WRITE has a "wordwrap" feature that automatically enters a carriage return and wraps the word that overflows to the next line.

The next section of the letter includes columnar data. Use the TAB key to enter the data. Remember, T marks a normal tab and D marks a decimal tab on the status line. Notice the difference that normal and decimal tabs make as you enter data. Use the decimal tab to enter the prices, entering the dollar sign first. When you add the salutation at the end, be sure to use the normal tab and not the decimal tab.

Adult	$15.00 one-way
	$25.00 round-trip
Children	$10.00 one-way
(5-11)	$15.00 round-trip
Child	(no cost)
(under 5)	
Senior Citizen	$12.00 one-way
	$21.00 round-trip

Trips leave Portland daily at 8:00 a.m. and 1 p.m. Each round-trip cruise lasts four hours. Enclosed is a brochure with further information. We look forward to having you sail with us.

Sincerely,

Adam Long
Sales Manager

st
Enclosure

EDITING THE DOCUMENT

Once you have entered the complete letter, you may return to it and make all of your corrections at one time. To do this, you will need a few additional keys. You have already discovered that various keys on the keyboard serve specific functions. Many of these functions are useful for editing documents. These functions are similar in all Software Publishing products, thus making it easy to go from one product to another. You do not have to learn a collection of new keyboard functions when beginning each program. Table 2-1 summarizes the keyboard functions for PFS:WRITE.

Experiment with the CURSOR CONTROL keys as you edit the letter you just entered. As mentioned earlier, any time you are entering or correcting text you can use the CURSOR CONTROL keys to move the cursor. If this does not work on your IBM PC, you may have pressed the NUM LOCK key. Press NUM LOCK again and see if the CURSOR CONTROL keys work. (Refer again to Figure 1-1 if you need help in locating keys). You

Table 2-1.   *PFS:WRITE Keyboard Functions*

Key	Function
F1	Brings up the help menu for **PFS:WRITE**
F2	Sets tabs
F3	Moves cursor to previous word
CTRL/F3	Moves cursor to beginning of line
F4	Moves cursor to next word
CTRL/F4	Moves cursor to previous word
F5	Labels a block
CTRL/F5	Erases a word
F6	Duplicates a block
CTRL/F6	Erases a line
F7	Initiates a search
CTRL/F7	Sets up for underlining
F8	Formats a line
CTRL/F8	Sets up for boldface
F9	Appends text
F10	Continues the current function
ESC	Cancels an operation and returns the user to the Main Menu
TAB	Moves the cursor to options on a menu and to the next tab stop in the text
SHIFT/TAB	Moves the cursor backward on a menu
BACKSPACE	Moves the cursor one position left and erases the last character you typed
CURSOR CONTROL	Moves the cursor one space in the direction of the arrow without erasing characters
INS	Acts as a toggle to switch you between insert and normal mode. When new characters are entered in insert mode, other characters move to the right to make spaces for them. In normal mode, any character entered overtypes any current character at that location
DEL	Deletes the character under the cursor location. Other characters are moved over to recover the space
PG DN	Brings up the next screen of a document on a multiple page document
PG UP	Brings up the previous screen of a document
HOME	Moves the cursor to the beginning of a document
END	Moves the cursor to the end of the document

Note: The SHIFT key can replace the CTRL key for any of the CTRL/key operations.
Two overlays, included with **PFS:WRITE**, can be used with the **IBM PC** function keys.

can also use the HOME key to move the cursor to the beginning of your document or the END key to move the cursor to the end of the document. The PG UP key moves the cursor 21 lines upward at a time, and the PG DN key moves the cursor down 21 lines at a time. These keys are useful for moving through the document a display page at a time. If the NUM LOCK key has been set for numeric entry, you will need to use the SHIFT key with HOME, END, PG UP and PG DN to get these functions to work.

At the left of the keyboard are the function keys. You have already learned about the F10 key. The F1 key (Help) can be used to get help at any time, but the program disk must be in the default drive. Try pressing the F1 key and see the screen displayed. Press the F10 key and you will be returned to your document. The help screen you see at any time depends upon the menu displayed. As an experiment, try different functions from the Main Menu, and when different menu screens are displayed, press F1 to see the help screen. You can always return to the function menu by pressing F10 and return to the Main Menu by pressing ESC.

You have also learned about the F2 key, which you used to set tabs. F1, F2, F9, and F10 each have only one function. The other keys each have two functions, depending upon whether or not they are used with the CTRL key. F3, for example, can be used to move the cursor left one word at a time. F4, in contrast, moves the cursor right one word at a time. If F3 is used with the CTRL key, the cursor moves to the beginning of the line it is on. If F4 is used with the CTRL key, the cursor moves to the end of the line. The SHIFT key can be used instead of the CTRL key with each of these to perform the same function. The other function keys will be discussed in Chapter 3.

You can insert characters at any point in your document to make changes. Move the cursor to the point in the document you wish to insert text. Do not worry about what you insert; the next paragraph shows you how to delete these same characters. Press the INS key. Notice that the cursor has changed from a blinking underscore to a blinking rectangle. The message "Inserting" appears on the status line. Now type the material you wish to insert. Once you have completed your insertion, press INS again. Notice that the word "Inserting" disappears from the status line.

To delete characters, move the cursor to the first character you wish to delete. Press DEL, and you will see the character disappear and the other characters shift to the left to recover the space. If you continue to press DEL, additional characters will be deleted.

If you wish to change any characters in the text without deletion or insertion, simply move the cursor to that place and type over the existing characters. Often it is easiest to combine operations, typing over some characters and inserting or deleting other characters.

Continue in this way. Add more text, correct your typing errors, and alter the text to learn the PFS:WRITE editing commands. You can also use F5 with the CTRL key to delete words and F6 with the CTRL key to delete lines. Once your document is edited, you can change the appearance of the text at any time by using the PFS:WRITE formatting capabilities.

FORMATTING THE DOCUMENT

The formatter permits you to control the margins and the page length. A document can be formatted and printed with one set of margins, and the margins can be changed and the document printed with a different set of margins. Both headers and footers can be inserted. A *header* is a line (or lines) of text that appears at the top of each page. A good example in a book manuscript is a title line that includes the author's name and address. A *footer* is a line that appears at the bottom of each page. For example, page numbers are footers. How to add headers and footers to your documents will be explained in the next chapter.

The PFS:WRITE formatter has basically two limitations. First, the right margin is limited to a maximum of 78. The default positions are a left margin of 10 and a right margin of 70. Default positions refer to the settings PFS:WRITE already has when it is first loaded and before any changes have been made. Second, right-justification is limited to single lines or columns of numbers, and these lines will not be left-justified. In other words, you can only justify a line at a time and a line can only be right- *or* left-justified.

Our sample letter was formatted as it was entered using the default values. Suppose, for example, you wished to change the margins. From the Main Menu, select function **2** (Define Page) and press F10. You will then see the Define Page Menu (Figure 2-3) with the cursor at the prompt for the "LEFT MARGIN:". Enter a new value of **15** and press F10. The margins on your document are reset to the new value. The document appears on the screen just as it will be printed. Now, put the margins back to the original values. To do this, press ESC to return to the Main Menu and select function **2** (Define Page) again. Press F10. When the Define Page Menu is displayed, enter **10** next to the "LEFT MARGIN:" prompt and press F10. The document should look as it did before the margins were changed.

You may wish to add various printing enhancements to your text to improve its readability. With PFS:WRITE, you can choose to boldface portions of your text or to add underlining. In this next exercise the Search function is used to locate text and boldface and underline enhancements are added to it.

Suppose you wanted to place "Willamette River Cruises" in boldface. First use the HOME key to return the cursor to the beginning of the document. Press F7 to initiate a search request, and enter **Willamette** as the word. Leave the request for "REPLACE WITH:" blank:

SEARCH FOR: **Willamette**
REPLACE WITH: MANUAL OR AUTOMATIC (M/A): **M**

Press F10 to initiate the search. The cursor will move and stop at the beginning of the word "Willamette" in the text. Press the CTRL and F8 keys. Notice that the first letter of the word is now in boldface on your screen. Pressing CTRL and F8 again will shift the next letter to boldface. Continue until the entire phrase is in boldface. Move the cursor backward a letter or two, and you will see that the status area at the bottom of the screen indicates the words are in boldface. The words are also displayed in boldface on the screen.

If you wish to underline a word, the same method is used, but this time the F7 key is pressed. Suppose you wish to underline the words "Willamette River Cruises" instead of using boldface. Use F7 to locate "Willamette" in the text. Type over the phrase to remove the boldface that you placed in the previous exercise. Put the cursor back to the first letter of the phrase. Now press the CTRL and F7 keys. If you are using a monochrome display, the text will be underscored on the screen. If you are using a color monitor, the underlined portion will be in a different color than the rest of the text. Press CTRL and F7 repeatedly until the entire phrase is underlined. Now move the cursor back a few letters and see that the status area changes to indicate the word is underlined. Once a word is marked for boldface or underscore, it will always show this on the screen unless you remove the enhancement.

SAVING THE DOCUMENT

You have completed your letter and now must save it to disk. If you turn your computer off and have not saved the document, you will lose it. After a document is created and edited, always save the document to a disk from which it can be retrieved and used at a later time. It is also a good practice to save every 15 or 30 minutes if you are entering a long document. Imagine spending hours entering a document, only to lose the work when "something happened." If the document had been saved periodically, only a small part of it would be lost.

To save your document, you need the data disk you formatted at the beginning of the chapter. Do *not* exit PFS:WRITE from the Main Menu to format a disk at this time, since your document has not been saved and it will be lost. Also, do not use your PFS:WRITE program disk to save the document.

To save your document, you must first return to the Main Menu. Press ESC and you will see the Main Menu again. Select function 4 (Get/Save/Remove) from this menu and press F10. You will then see the Get/Save/Remove Menu shown in Figure 2-5. Select option 2 (Save Document) from this menu to save your document. (Remember, selections from the Main Menu are called *functions* and selections from other menus are called *options*.)

You will now have to give your document a name that will be used as a file name to store the document on the disk. This must be a unique name; that is, no other document on the disk can have this name. Call this document TEST.LTR. Use TAB to move to the file name query and enter this name next to "DIRECTORY OR FILE NAME:". Be sure to use any necessary disk designator. For example, if your data disk is in Drive B, enter **B:TEST.LTR**. You can use upper- or lowercase letters, since the program will automatically capitalize your entry. When you

```
                        GET/SAVE/REMOVE MENU




                    1   GET DOCUMENT

                    2   SAVE DOCUMENT

                    3   REMOVE FILE



                    SELECTION NUMBER: 2

                    DIRECTORY OR FILE NAME: B:TEST.LTR

F1-Help                                               F10-Continue
```

Figure 2-5.   The Get/Save/Remove Menu

have completed your selection, press F10. The document will then be saved to the disk.

If you wish to edit this letter later and print it again, you can use this same Get/Save/Remove Menu to get a document or letter. You can try this now to see if you saved your document successfully. Select function 5 (Clear) from the Main Menu and press F10 to clear the working document in memory. This does not erase the document on the disk, but only clears it from the computer memory. Then from the Main Menu select function 4 (Get/Save/Remove) and press F10 to get the document. When this menu is displayed, enter option 1 (Get Document) and the file name **B:TEST.LTR**. Press F10; this will retrieve the document with the tab settings intact.

Unlike many word processors, PFS:WRITE does *not* automatically create a backup copy (duplicate) of your document each time you edit a document that already exists on the disk. Backup copies are essential insurance against losing or destroying your files. To create backup copies, use the copy utility that is a part of the operating system, and copy your document file to a separate disk. Another way to back up your document would be to save the document with the Get/Save/Remove Menu a second time under a different file name.

PRINTING THE DOCUMENT

The final step in this tutorial is the actual printing of the document. The PFS:WRITE program can print your document with almost any type of printer that can be used with the IBM PC. In addition to underlining and boldface, you can also send special codes to the printer from PFS:WRITE. These can be used to change the character spacing, line spacing (single or double), or otherwise control the printer. You can, with a few tricks, do subscripts and superscripts (see Chapter 3).

PFS:WRITE prints the document from the computer memory, not from a file on the disk. This is somewhat dangerous, since you could print a document and forget to save it. Develop the habit of saving your document before you print it. Since the sample letter is still in the computer memory, the document can now be printed. If the document was not in computer memory, you would first load the document from the disk using the Get Document option from the Get/Save/Remove Menu.

To print the document, select function 3 (Print) from the Main Menu. You will then see the Print Menu, shown in Figure 2-6. You may change any of these default values if you wish before printing. The

```
                    PRINT MENU

          FROM PAGE: 1    TO PAGE: 1

          PRINT TO: LPT1:

          PAUSE BETWEEN PAGES (Y/N): N

          NUMBER OF COPIES: 1

          SINGLE/DOUBLE/ENVELOPE (S/D/E): S

          INDENT: 0

          JOINING PFS:GRAPH (Y/N): N

          PFS FILE NAME:



  F1-Help                                        F10-Continue
```

Figure 2-6.   *The Print Menu*

Print To option is the only option you will use now. The other options are explained in Chapter 3.

The Print To option determines which device the printed output will be directed to. You can use serial or parallel printers, but you cannot direct the output to the console. The default value is the parallel printer (LPT1:). If you have a serial printer, refer to Appendix C. The Print To option is also used if you wish to "print" the document to a disk file. This is useful if you are creating a document that will be sent to a publisher or typesetter on a disk and you wish a final, formatted copy on the disk that can be used by other programs. This feature will be explained further in Chapter 12.

Leave all options at their default values unless you have a serial printer and press F10. You will then see on the screen

POSITION THE PAPER IN YOUR PRINTER

Press F10 to continue

Be sure your printer is on and ready and then press F10 a second time. The document will then print. The printed document appears as shown in Figure 2-4.

LEAVING PFS:WRITE

When you have finished creating and printing the documents, press ESC to return to the Main Menu. Select function **6** (Exit) and press F10. This will return you to your computer's operating system, and you will see the operating system prompt:

A>

From this prompt, you can enter the name of any other program you wish to use.

CHAPTER
THREE

Using Advanced Features
Of PFS:WRITE

You have already learned how to create and print a simple letter using
PFS:WRITE. Now you probably want to try some of the more advanced
features, such as block editing, search and replace, envelope formatting,
and special printing enhancements. In this chapter you will learn how
to use all these advanced features.

BLOCK EDITING

Block editing allows you to move, delete, or duplicate an entire block of
text. With PFS:WRITE, blocks of text can be deleted, copied to another
section in the same document or to another document, or deleted from
one area and moved to another place in the same document or to
another document. You first mark or label the block and then initiate
the action.

As an exercise, return to the document you created in Chapter 2. Load
PFS:WRITE, select function 4 (Get/Save/Remove) from the Main
Menu, and press F10. From the Get/Save/Remove Menu, select option 1

(Get Document), enter the file name **B:TEST.LTR** next to "DIREC-TORY OR FILE NAME:", and press F10 again. You will then see the letter displayed. Move the cursor to the beginning of the last paragraph in the text (beginning with "Trips") and press F5. The first letter of the paragraph is highlighted. You will also notice the status line now indicates "labeling." Press ENTER twice and move the cursor just beyond the period following the word "information." The three sentences are now highlighted, since each line is highlighted as ENTER is pressed. You have now marked (or labeled) the three sentences as a block (see Figure 3-1). The next key you press will determine whether the block will be deleted, copied, or moved, or whether the operation will be aborted. There are four valid key entries:

F5   Abort the block operation; remain in the document
ESC   Abort the operation; return to the Main Menu
DEL   Delete or move the block
F6   Copy the block to another location (duplicate block)

Once a block has been defined, using the CURSOR CONTROL keys to move to the beginning of the block will abort the operation. Remember,

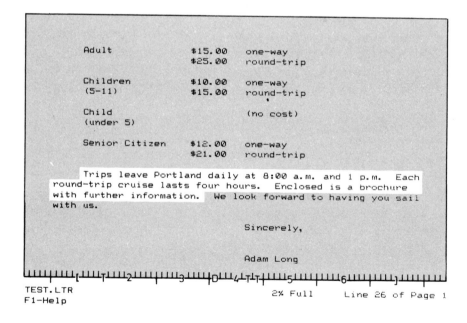

Figure 3-1. Marking a block of text

to begin a block operation, mark a block by moving the cursor to the beginning of the block and press F5. Use the CURSOR CONTROL keys to move the cursor to the end of the block and press a key to indicate the type of operation to be performed on the block. Sentences, phrases, or paragraphs can be defined as blocks and moved, deleted, or copied in this way. This example defined three sentences as a block. Before proceeding, press F5 again to abort the operation. The sentences are no longer highlighted.

Move the cursor to the first letter of the last paragraph, which begins with "Trips". Press F5, and then press ENTER twice to move the cursor after the period following the word "information" to highlight the three sentences.

Now press DEL, and you will see the three sentences vanish from your text. They are not really gone. They are stored in the *block buffer,* a special buffer area in the computer memory. The text will remain in this buffer until another block of text is written to the buffer or until you exit PFS:WRITE. Move the cursor backward in the letter until it is on the first character of the second sentence in the text that begins "The cruises ...". Press F6 and you will see the three sentences magically appear.

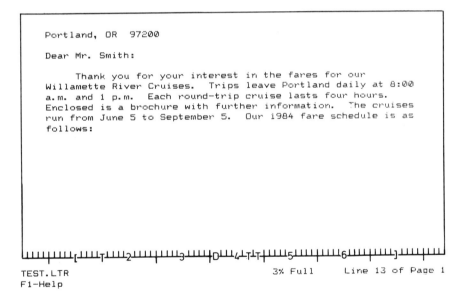

```
    Portland, OR  97200

    Dear Mr. Smith:

        Thank you for your interest in the fares for our
    Willamette River Cruises.  Trips leave Portland daily at 8:00
    a.m. and 1 p.m.  Each round-trip cruise lasts four hours.
    Enclosed is a brochure with further information.  The cruises
    run from June 5 to September 5.  Our 1984 fare schedule is as
    follows:
```

```
TEST.LTR                          3% Full      Line 13 of Page 1
F1-Help
```

The three sentences are still in the block buffer and can even be moved to another document. To do this, press ESC to return to the Main

Menu, enter function 5 (Clear), and press F10 to clear the document from your computer memory. You will see a warning that you are erasing an altered document. Ignore the warning and press F10 again. You will then be returned to the edit screen, which is now blank, since the document has been cleared from memory. Press F6; you will see the two sentences again since changing documents does not clear the block buffer. This method can be used to delete text from one document and to add the same text to another document. Before continuing, reload your document by pressing ESC, entering function 4 (Get/Save/Remove), pressing F10, and selecting 1 (Get Document) from the Get/Save/Remove Menu. Now enter the file name **B:TEST.LTR** and press F10.

Deleting a block is similar to moving it to another document except you do not use F6 to reenter the block at another location. The block is still moved to the block buffer. This is a handy feature, since you may later decide to restore the text to the same file. By using F6 you can retrieve the same block and return it to the text. Try it now with the same three sentences. Mark your document block again, and use the DEL key to remove the block. The block is now deleted. Before continuing, restore the document to its original text again by pressing F6.

Copying a block is almost the same as moving a block, but you do not delete the block from its original location. Try this now with the same three sentences. Mark the same block, leaving the cursor at the end of the sentence that ends with "information." This time press F6 instead of DEL. Notice that the paragraph remains on the screen and is not highlighted.

A copy of the first four sentences has been placed in the block buffer. Now again move the cursor to the sentence that begins "The cruises ..." and enter F6 a second time. The marked sentences will still be at both their original location and the new location.

To review block operations, see Figure 3-2. Remember, after the block is marked, use DEL or F6 to delete, copy, or move the block.

Using the JOIN Command

There is one limitation on block moves and copies. The maximum size of a block that can be moved or copied is limited to the size of the block buffer, which is about 35 lines of text. If you try to move more than this, you will get a message on the screen saying that your block is too large. You can, however, delete any size block. If you need to copy a large block of text between documents, you should use the JOIN command.

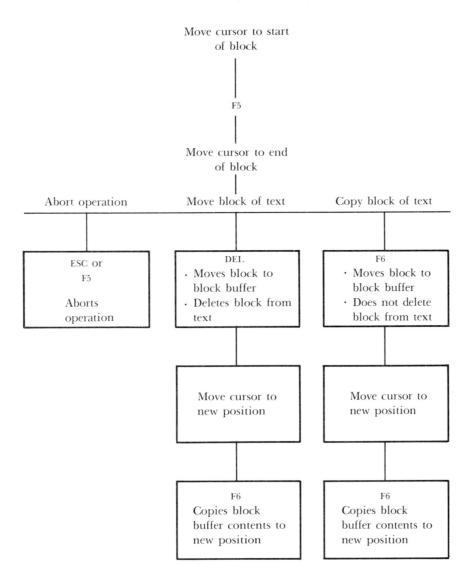

Figure 3-2. *Block move operations*

For example, suppose you wished to send the letter you just created as a form letter to several people. In each letter you wish to add a paragraph to personalize the letter and refer to a specific point. In each letter you will change one paragraph as well as the name and address. With PFS:WRITE the work is easily performed using the JOIN command. For example, the part of the letter that is common to each recipient is

first created with PFS:WRITE and later saved as a file. Using the letter
TEST.LTR, delete all but the body of the letter, so that TEST.LTR
contains only the following text:

Thank you for your interest in the fares for our
Willamette River Cruises. The cruises run from June 5 to
September 5. Our 1984 fare schedule is as follows:

Adult	$15.00 one-way
	$25.00 round-trip
Children	$10.00 one-way
(5-11)	$15.00 round-trip
Child	(no cost)
(under 5)	
Senior Citizen	$12.00 one-way
	$21.00 round-trip

Trips leave Portland daily at 8:00 A.M. and 1:00 P.M. Each
round-trip cruise lasts four hours. Enclosed is a brochure
with further information. We look forward to having you sail
with us.

Now save this letter body as B:TEMP.LTR by entering ESC, selecting
function 4 (Get/Save/Remove), pressing F10, and selecting function 2
(Save Document) from the Get/Save/Remove Menu. Change the file
name on this menu to **B:TEMP.LTR**. The file you have just saved
would be called a *template letter* by word processing specialists; it is a
master letter or form that is used to create several letters. Now enter
function 5 (Clear) from the Main Menu to clear the work area and enter
a date, address, and greeting.

February 28, 1984

Mr. John Smith
22400 SW Milwaukie Way
Portland, OR 97200

Dear Mr. Smith:

Enter the JOIN command line as follows:

JOIN B:TEMP.LTR

Add the following personal paragraph:

    You requested specific information on our special spring
    holiday trip. At the present time this is completely
    booked, but we will add your name to the waiting list
    and notify you if there is an opening.
                        Sincerely,

                        Adam Long
                        Sales Manager

st
Enclosure

Press ESC and print this letter. The body of the letter will be read from the disk and added to the document with the original margins when the document is printed. The text you are joining (the body of the letter) will not show on the screen while you are editing the final letter (adding the date, address, salutation, or paragraph), but when the letter is printed, **PFS:WRITE** will access this common text (TEMP.LTR) and print it at the marked place. Be sure to use any disk drive designator (such as B:) if the text is not from the same disk drive as your program. (Word processing specialists use the term *boilerplating* to refer to the process of obtaining text from another file at print time. Lawyers and other professionals often create a large collection of boilerplating text files to use in their work.) You can also abbreviate the JOIN command as follows:

J B:TEST.LTR

Now print the letter by pressing ESC to return to the Main Menu and select function **3** (Print). Press F10 three times.

USING SEARCH AND REPLACE

In Chapter 2, you used the Search function to locate the word "Willamette" in your text. In this section you will learn some additional features of the Search function and will also learn how to use the Replace function.

Reload the sample letter and locate the word "Willamette" again. Remember to use the HOME key to move the cursor to the beginning of the screen. Then use F7 to start the search operation. The screen will display a request for the search string:

SEARCH FOR:
REPLACE WITH: MANUAL OR AUTOMATIC (M/A): M

Enter **Willamette** next to "SEARCH FOR:" and press F10. The cursor will move to the word "Willamette" in the text, stopping at the first character of the word. The characters you enter next to the "SEARCH FOR:" prompt are called the *search phrase* and represent the string that must be matched in the text. The search phrase can be entered in upper- or lowercase letters, and a match will be found regardless of the case of the word in the text; "Willamette" will match both "Willamette" and "WILLAMETTE." The Search function observes the following rules in matching the phrase you enter:

- Upper- and lowercases are ignored.
- If the search phrase involves more than two words, anything more than one space between the words is ignored. For example, "a test" for a search phrase will match both "a test" and "a test".
- Spaces before or after the search phrase are ignored. For example, " as " is identical to "as".

There are times when you may wish to search using only a part of a word or phrase. For example, you may wish to find "inclosed" in your text, and you are not sure whether you spelled it "inclosed" or "enclosed." PFS:WRITE recognizes the ".." as a special symbol to indicate unknown characters in your search phrase. Press HOME and then F7 and find the word by requesting the following search:

SEARCH FOR: ..closed

This will find any word ending in "closed," regardless of the length of the word. Press F10. If a search scan stops too soon because it found a match before the match you wanted, you continue the scan by pressing F10 again. As a general rule, you will always want to start your scan from the beginning of the document, so you will need to press HOME before starting your search request.

The symbols used for partial matches (..) can also be used at the end of a phrase to match unknown characters. For example, "Wil.." would match any word beginning in "Wil." You can also use the symbols at both the beginning and end of a word. For example you could enter "..xam.." to find "example."

The replace operation is very similar to the search operation. In this case, however, you will want to enter a value in response to the "REPLACE WITH:" prompt on the screen.

For example, in the letter, change the word "four" to "from four to five." Press the HOME key to move the cursor to the beginning of the text, and then press F7 to initiate the search operation. Enter **four** as the search phrase, and enter **four to five** as the replacement value. Press F10 and the cursor will move to the first occurrence of "four" in the text. You will then see a prompt requesting whether you wish the word changed. Enter **Y**. The word will change, and if necessary the lines of the text will be readjusted.

As you initiate a Search or Replace function, you will see a prompt on the lower right of the screen that requests

MANUAL OR AUTOMATIC (Y/N)?

In the examples so far you have not responded, so the Replace function defaulted to a manual mode. In this mode the Replace function stops on each searched phrase and queries whether or not you want to replace it. In some cases, you may wish to replace all matches automatically without stopping for the query. In this case you would TAB to the question and enter a **Y** for the automatic mode. After initiating the replacement, all matches will be replaced with no stops for queries. Use this *very* cautiously, as it is easy to inadvertently replace something you did not intend to replace. To practice, move the cursor again to the beginning of the text (use the HOME key) and enter **..a..** as the search phrase. Enter **abcdefghijk** as the replacement phrase. TAB to the "MANUAL OR AUTOMATIC (M/A):" query, enter an **A**, and press F10. Watch what happens. To get a fresh copy of your document again, select the Get function from the Get/Save/Remove Menu.

Another interesting feature of search and replace operations allows you to count the occurrences of a specific word or phrase in the text. To see this work, use F7 to initiate a search and enter the search phrase **four** as before. Leave the replacement phrase blank, and use automatic mode. When the scan is completed, the number of times the phrase appeared in the text will be displayed. You might use this feature to check for the overuse of certain phrases in your document if you suspect certain words have been overworked. You could then use the Search and Replace functions to change one or more of these to another phrase.

FORMATTING

Formatting organizes text for printing and screen display. In this section you will learn how to justify lines of text, execute special print features, make new pages, add headers and footers, and select most of the Print Menu features. You will find it easy to perform all of these operations on the sample letter. As you recall from Chapter 2, *justification* is the process of aligning text with a margin. If text is right-justified, the right edges of all lines of text form a straight vertical line like the printed page of a book. Text can also be left-justified and center-justified. This is used to center titles or headings. Although PFS:WRITE can do right- and center-justification, it can only do it one line at a time. In addition, you cannot justify both left and right margins of a single line of text. *This means you will always have either a ragged right or ragged left margin.* For letters and correspondence, you might prefer a ragged right margin, since a letter with this format looks less like a computer printout and more like something created by a human being.

Try to left-justify the date in the TEST.LTR document you created earlier. Move the cursor to the beginning of the date line and press F8. You will then see the prompt

LEFT CENTER RIGHT (L/C/R)?

Enter an **L** and you will see the date return to the left margin. Now try to center the date on the line. Press F8 again and enter a **C** this time. You will see the date move to the center of the line. Justification is always immediate and can be changed again at any time. A line is always left-justified when it is entered.

There is one other form of justification that will be discussed in Chapter 11. It is used to read data from a file created with PFS:FILE and align it with data that is already in your document.

Using Special Print Features

Using the PRINTER command, you can use PFS:WRITE to print subscripts, superscripts, double-wide characters, or special fonts. In fact, you can set up the printer for any format just by sending it the proper codes. You can switch the print style in the middle of a line of text to print in a different font and switch it back after a word or phrase is printed. To do this, you will need to read your printer's user manual to find the appropriate codes for your printer. Locate the decimal codes for the desired function. Do not use the hexadecimal codes. For example, for the Okidata 93 printer, the following is a list of codes for several functions. Many of these functions will be used in this section and the next. *Emphasized printing* means printing the same text twice with the second printing offset horizontally from the first printing to give a boldface effect. *Enhanced printing* means printing the same text twice with the second printing offset vertically to give a boldface effect. Notice that in some cases it is necessary to use two codes to initiate a function.

Emphasized printing	(turn on)	27,84
Enhanced printing	(turn on)	27,72
Emphasized and enhanced printing	(turn off)	27,73
Double-wide printing		31
10 characters per inch (elite)		30
12 characters per inch (pica)		28
17 characters per inch (condensed)		29
Superscripts	(turn on)	27,74
	(turn off)	27,75
Subscripts	(turn on)	27,76
	(turn off)	27,77

Locate the same functions in your printer's manual and note the appropriate decimal codes or code sequences to initiate these functions. Some of these functions may not be available on some printers. If this is true with your printer, skip the related tutorial or modify the example for the codes that are available.

The next example prints a short piece with enhanced and double-wide letters for the title. Clear your work area by pressing ESC, function 5 (Clear), and pressing F10 twice. Select function 1 (Type/Edit) from the Main Menu and enter the opening printer codes, text, and closing printer codes. The PRINTER command is used to initiate the code sequence. The command must start *and* stop with asterisks. Be sure to use the proper codes for your printer. Use a *space* before the first number in the PRINTER command and a *comma* between adjacent numbers. After the title is printed, the printer is switched to its normal style of 10 character per inch mode without the enhanced print. Be sure to use the codes for your printer if they are different from the following:

PRINTER 31,27,72
NEWS RELEASE!
PRINTER 30,27,73

Now type in the news release copy.

April 2, 1984

A new communications software product, SUPERCOM, is now available for information utility users from Computer Software. Designed especially for electronic communication applications, SUPERCOM includes features for accessing systems that support electronic mail, bulletin boards, and electronic conferencing.

After this text is entered, press ESC, and select function 3 (Print). Be sure your printer is turned on, and press F10 twice. The final printed news release is shown in Figure 3-3. Before continuing, be sure to save the document. Select function 4 (Get/Save/Remove) from the Main Menu and press F10. On the Get/Save/Remove Menu select option 2 (Save Document) and enter the file name **B:NEWS.DOC**. Press F10, and the document will be saved.

Let's now create a short document that demonstrates how to use superscripts. We will use this same document later to illustrate the NEW PAGE command and headers and footers. From the Main Menu select function 5 (Clear) to clear the screen and press F10. You may need to press F10 again to complete the clearing and return to the Main Menu. Now select function 1 (Type/Edit) and press F10. Enter the fol-

```
   NEWS  RELEASE !

April 2, 1984

A new communications software product, SUPERCOM, is now
available for information utility users from Computer
Software.  Designed especially for electronic communication
applications, SUPERCOM includes features for accessing
information utility systems  that support electronic mail,
bulletin boards, and electronic conferencing.
```

Figure 3-3.   *Printing double-wide enhanced characters*

lowing document, which is the opening paragraphs from a paper on the history of word processing:

The History of Word Processing

The typewriter was invented in 1867 by Christopher Sholes, Carlos Glidden, and S.D. Soule.*p 27,74*1*p 27,75* The first typewriter on the market was produced by Remington and Sons in 1874. Although Edison invented the dictating machine in the early twentieth century, the first electric typewriter did not appear until the 1920s.

The title can be centered with the F8 key (see Chapter 2). Notice that we have now abbreviated the **PRINTER** command to a single "p" followed by the appropriate codes. (This can be upper- or lowercase.) Be very careful to limit the **PRINTER** command to one line. All of the information between the asterisks *must* be on the same line. Also be sure to include *both* asterisks. Use the printer codes listed in your printer's manual to turn the superscripts on and off. Once the text has been entered, press ESC to return to the Main Menu, select function **3** (Print), and press F10 to print your document. The printout should look like Figure 3-4.

```
       The History of Word Processing

The typewriter was invented in 1867 by Christopher Sholes,
Carlos Glidden, and S.D. Soule.1  The first typewriter on the
market was produced by Remington and Sons in 1874.  Although
Edison invented the dictating machine in the early twentieth
century, the first electric typewriter did not appear until
the 1920s.
```

Figure 3-4.   *Printing superscripts*

Another example of a print command is the NEW PAGE command. At times you may want to specify exactly where a new page should begin. To do this, use the following command:

NEW PAGE

This command instructs the printer to perform a form feed and start a new page in your document. You can abbreviate the command by entering **N** in a line of text as follows:

N

For example, add the NEW PAGE command to the document just created and another superscript with the reference. Select function 1 (Type/Edit) from the Main Menu and press F10. The document should now be displayed. Move the cursor to the end of the text by pressing END and then add the NEW PAGE command and the reference:

The History of Word Processing

The typewriter was invented in 1867 by Christopher Sholes, Carlos Glidden, and S.D. Soule.*p 27,74*1*p 27,75* The first typewriter on the market was produced by Remington and Sons in 1874. Although Edison invented the dictating machine in the early twentieth century, the first electric typewriter did not appear until the 1920s.
N
*p 27,74*1*p 27,75* Townsend, Carl, *Exploring Word Processors: CP/M Edition* (dilithium Press, 1984) p. 38

Refer to Chapter 2 if you need help with underlining text (use the CTRL/F7 keys). After you have entered the text, press ESC to return to the Main Menu, select function 3 (Print), and press F10 three times to print the document. Finally, select function 4 (Get/Save/Remove) and press F10 to save the document. Select option 2 (Save Document), enter the document name as **B:WP.DOC**, and press F10 to complete the saving of the document. Do not clear the document from the screen (function 5), as you will continue using it in the next section.

Using Headers and Footers

On certain documents you may wish to put a header or footer. A *header* is a line (or lines) of text that appear(s) at the top of every page. If you are writing a manuscript or article, you will probably want your name and address on the top of every page. If you are writing a report, you may wish to have your report title and perhaps a date at the top of every page. A footer is not a footnote. (A footnote appears on only one page and will move if the reference to the footnote changes.) A *footer* is a line (or lines) of text that appears at the bottom of every page. An example would be the page number. You can do both headers and footers with PFS:WRITE.

As an exercise, add a header and footer to the document created in the last section. It should still be in the computer work area, since you did not clear the work area. Select function **2** (Define Page) from the Main Menu and press F10. You will see the Define Page Menu (Figure 3-5). In

```
                        DEFINE PAGE MENU




            LEFT MARGIN: 10      RIGHT MARGIN: 70

            TOP  MARGIN: 6       BOTTOM MARGIN: 6

            PAGE LENGTH: 66




    HEADING: Gerald Wigglesby, 3075 Fairlane, Washington, D.C.  20002

    FOOTING: PAGE 1




    F1-Help                                        F10-Continue
```

Figure 3-5. *The Define Page Menu*

the lower half of the page there is a space to add two lines of header information or two lines of footer information.

HEADER:

FOOTER:

Enter your name and address as the HEADER, and for the FOOTER enter **PAGE 1** as follows:

HEADER: Gerald Wigglesby, 3075 Fairlane, Washington, D.C. 20002
FOOTER: PAGE 1

Page numbering can be initiated by entering any number to the footer prompt. For example, if you enter **PAGE 1** as the footer on the Define Page Menu, the numeric value is assumed to be a page number and will be incremented on subsequent pages. You could also omit the word "Page" and use only the number if desired. Both headers and footers will be centered on the page.

Now press F10 to return to the Main Menu, select function **3** (Print), and press F10. Be sure the printer is on and press F10 again. Your document should now be printed with the header and footer. Save the document by selecting function **4** (Get/Save/Remove) from the Main Menu and pressing F10. Select option **2** (Save Document) from the Get/Save/Remove Menu and enter the file name as **B:WP.DOC** again. As you will be overwriting the document **B:WP.DOC** that you saved earlier, you will need to press F10 a second time to save the document after you see the warning screen.

PRINT MENU FEATURES

Several print features can be selected from the Print Menu just before a document is printed. The document used in the preceding example should still be in the work area of your computer. From the Main Menu, select function **3** (Print) and press F10. You will then see the Print Menu shown in Figure 3-6. Using the options displayed, you can control what part of the document to print, how to print the document, and where the computer should send the output. Here is a brief overview of these features:

```
                    PRINT MENU

        FROM PAGE: 1   TO PAGE: 1

        PRINT TO: LPT1:

        PAUSE BETWEEN PAGES (Y/N): N

        NUMBER OF COPIES: 1

        SINGLE/DOUBLE/ENVELOPE (S/D/E): S

        INDENT: 0

        JOINING PFS:GRAPH (Y/N): N

        PFS FILE NAME:



        F1-Help                              F10-Continue
```

Figure 3-6.   *The Print Menu*

From Page: and To Page:	Starts and ends the printing from any point in the document. Used to print only a portion of a document. This is useful if the printer jams while printing a document; you can print just the part where the printer jammed. This is also useful to print only the portion of a document that you edited.
Print To:	Specifies which device the output will be directed to. You can use serial or parallel printers, but you cannot direct the output to the console. The default value prints to the parallel printer (LPT1:). This option is also used to "print" the document to a disk file.
Pause Between Pages:	Stops the printer between pages to allow time to insert letterhead stationery.

Number of Copies:	Selects how many copies of each page you wish to print.
Single/Double/Envelope (S/D/E):	Selects single or double spacing and automatically prints envelopes. Accepts only one option at a time.
Indent:	Controls the horizontal starting point for the page. It is easier to change this than to move the paper horizontally in the printer. Both left and right margins are shifted by the amount of the indent. The default value is zero.
Join PFS:GRAPH (Y/N)	Used to add a graph to your document. This option is discussed in Chapter 11.
PFS File Name:	Prints form letters using an address file created with PFS:FILE. This will be explained in Chapter 11. For now leave blank.

One of the most important options, the Print To option, which specifies the correct printer device or prints the document to a disk, requires further discussion. If you are using a parallel printer, this value should be the default value of LPT1:. If you have more than one parallel device on your computer system, a parallel printer might be LPT2:. If you have a serial printer, this value will be COM1: or COM2:. Enter the correct value when the Print Menu is displayed. You can also use this option to "print" your document to a floppy disk. This process creates an exact copy of the printed document that is saved as a file on the disk. Printing to a disk converts the file to standard characters that can be read by other word processors or utilities. This is useful for creating a copy of the document to use with another word processor or utility or to send a finished document to another computer. For example, you might submit an article on disk to a magazine publisher. The publisher could then typeset the article directly from your floppy disk, adding only the typesetting codes. This can be done from the Print Menu by changing the Print To option to the name of a disk file. Try this now by selecting function 3 (Print) from the Main Menu and pressing F10 to initiate the print as if you planned to print your document. When the Print Menu is displayed, use the TAB key to move the cursor to the Print To option and enter the name of the file that you wish for the output document. Again, be sure to use the appropriate disk designator:

PRINT TO: B:TEST.PRN

Press F10, and the document will be "printed" to the disk. This will work with any document that does not contain a chart from PFS:GRAPH, since only text files can be "printed" to a disk.

The Single/Double/Envelope (S/D/E): option also requires additional discussion. Double spacing is often used for first drafts that will be hand corrected. Try this now by using the Print Menu to print your letter with double spacing. Select function **3** (Print) from the Main Menu and press F10. On the Print Menu locate the Single/Double/Envelope (S/D/E): option. Enter a **D** for this option, press F10, and print your letter again.

Envelope Printing

PFS:WRITE has a very interesting feature: the address entered in the letter can be used to print an address on an envelope for a letter. Try this now with TEST.LTR. From the Main Menu, select function **4** (Get/Save/Remove) and press F10. Select option **1** (Get Document) and enter the name of the letter file as **B:TEST.LTR**. You already have the address that will be used for the envelope as a part of the letter. Select function **3** (Print) from the Main Menu and press F10. On the displayed Print Option Menu find the following information:

SINGLE/DOUBLE/ENVELOPE (S/D/E)?

Enter **E** for ENVELOPE next to this question and press F10 to get the message screen. Press F10 again to start the printer. The address will be printed 10 lines down and indented 35 spaces. If you wish to try it with an envelope, place the envelope in the printer with the printer head at the top left edge of the envelope.

PFS:WRITE finds the address for the envelope in your letter by scanning down the left margin, skipping any line that is not aligned with the left margin or any date line. (A *date line* is any line that ends with at least two digits.) The end point of the address is assumed to be the first blank line after the starting point. Recognizing this strategy, you should place your own return address in the upper right. The scanner will then skip your address and print only the recipient's address.

USING THE GET/SAVE/REMOVE MENU

You have already used two of the options on the Get/Save/Remove option in getting and saving files. In this section you will learn more about these options and learn how to remove documents from your disk.

The working document is always stored in the computer memory, and any document is printed from memory, *not* from a file on the disk as with most word processors. A document can be cleared from memory with function 5 (Clear) on the Main Menu. This does not, however, remove any disk file from the disk. If you never saved the document to the disk, using the Clear function or leaving PFS:WRITE using function 6 (Exit) will lose the document, and it can never be recovered. Always save the document you are working on (every fifteen or thirty minutes and periodically back up your document files) to prevent this loss of information. In this way, you can always get back to the last copy of the document you saved to the disk.

In this section you will retrieve a document you have already created that is on the disk, save it again under a new name, and finally remove the new copy of the document you created. In the process, you will learn a few new things about the Get/Save/Remove Menu.

Insert your data disk in drive B and select function 4 (Get/Save/ Remove) from the Main Menu to display the Get/Save/Remove Menu shown in Figure 3-7. Select option 1 on this menu (Get Document) and enter a disk file designator for the file name.

DIRECTORY OR FILE NAME: B:

Now press F10, and you will see a list of the files on your data disk and the prompt:

NAME OF DOCUMENT TO GET:

```
GET/SAVE/REMOVE MENU




        1   GET DOCUMENT

        2   SAVE DOCUMENT

        3   REMOVE FILE




        SELECTION NUMBER: 1

        DIRECTORY OR FILE NAME: B:



F1-Help                                                F10-Continue
```

Figure 3-7.   *The Get/Save/Remove Menu*

If the list of files is longer than one screen display, you will also see directions for scrolling the list to see the rest of the files using the PGUP and PGDN keys. Enter **B:TEST.LTR**, press F10, and your file will be retrieved and displayed for editing.

There are a few other special notes of interest about the Get option. It not only retrieves files created by PFS:WRITE, it also retrieves files created with other word processors if the text contains standard characters with no special coding. PFS:WRITE uses a special format in saving files, and files created with PFS:WRITE will load into memory faster with Get for editing than a file created by another editor or word processor. You may find that after loading a document created by another word processor you will have to edit the document or make other changes. Some word processors (such as WordStar) store the text in a rather unusual file format that cannot be read correctly by PFS:WRITE. If you use the other word processor to *print* a document to a disk, the resulting file will contain only standard characters and can be read by PFS:WRITE using the Get function. This will be more completely discussed in Chapter 12.

To save the document now in the computer memory under a new

name, press ESC to return to the Main Menu, select function **4** (Get/Save/Remove) again, and press F10. The Get/Save/Remove Menu will be displayed again. Select option **2** (Save Document). You could, if you wished, enter the new name for the document. Suppose, however, you did not know what names were already in use on the disk? To examine existing file names, enter only the disk designator

DIRECTORY OR FILE NAME: B:

and press F10. You will then see the file names of the existing files on the disk and the prompt:

SAVE WORKING COPY AS:

Enter the new document name as **B:TEST2.LTR** and press F10. Your document will be saved. You now have two copies of your document on the disk. One of these is B:TEST.LTR and the second is B:TEST2.LTR.

Now remove the second copy of the document. Select function **4** (Get/Save/Remove) from the Main Menu and press F10. You will see the Get/Save/Remove Menu. From this menu select option **3** (Remove File) and enter the file name **B:TEST2.LTR**. Press F10, and you see the warning message that you are removing a file. Press F10 a second time, and the file will be removed. If you are not sure what files are on the disk, you could enter the disk drive designator B: for the file name and press F10 as you did to get and save the file in order to see a list of the files on the disk. You can always abort the remove process by pressing ESC to return to the Main Menu.

CHAPTER
FOUR

Using PFS:FILE

PFS:FILE is a file management system. It functions like a file system that uses index cards. PFS:FILE can manage information stored as a collection that is regularly referenced and updated. Examples include customer names and addresses, inventory, employee records, and time calendars. It is *not* a database management system and does not have the full conveniences of the more sophisticated database managers. It does, however, have enough flexibility and capability to meet the needs of many applications; it is inexpensive and easy to use.

INTRODUCING PFS:FILE

PFS:FILE can best be viewed as an electronic filing system for records. A *record* is a collection of information about a single person, a product, an event, or anything you like. These records are stored in *files*. For example, in a medical record file, information about each patient would be contained in one record. Information about these records is entered into forms, which can consist of one or more *pages*. A form allows orderly data entry and storage. The PFS:FILE manual uses the term *form* to refer to both the record and the form used to enter the record information. This book uses two different terms to clarify the distinction between the empty form (used to enter information) and the record (a completed form).

From one to thirty-two pages can be used for each record you store. The pieces of information stored in forms for each record are called *items*. Medical records, for example, might have these items: Name, Social Security Number, Address, City, State, ZIP Code, Home Phone, Insurance Program, and Insurance Number. You can use a maximum of 100 items on each displayed page and as many as 32 pages (see Figure 4-1).

PFS:FILE has some limitations. There are no mathematical computations, so if you are using PFS:FILE for inventory control, you will not be able to calculate the total value of your inventory. If you use PFS:FILE with PFS:REPORT, however, you can do some of the mathematical calculations you would need for inventory control. There

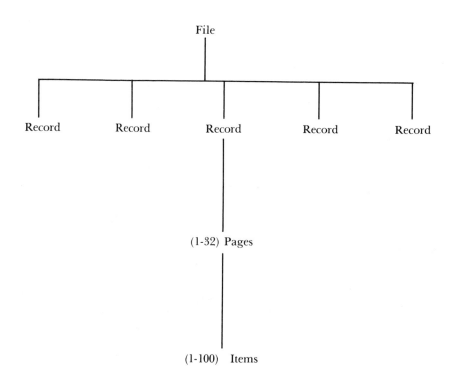

Figure 4-1. Organization of information in PFS:FILE

are also some limits to its sorting capability. You can extract records from one file based on any criteria and put them in another file. Sorting and selection is done by masking items for desired matches. A *mask* is a template value used in searches to find records that match any criteria. For example, you can find all records with a "b" in a name item or "Alameda" in a street address item. There are no logical operations such as AND, OR, and NOT that can be used in the selection process between two or more values for the same item. For example, you cannot find records using "97212 OR 97213" for a ZIP code item, but you could use "972??" to find all items with ZIP codes beginning with 972.

PFS:FILE has many of the same features PFS:WRITE has. You do not need to remember the name of a function to initiate it. All PFS:FILE functions are selected from a single Main Menu (see Figure 4-2). This menu is displayed when you start the program, making it easy to begin working.

You will also discover that various keys on the keyboard serve specific functions. Many of these functions are similar in all Software Publishing products, thus making it easy to go from one product to another without having to learn a collection of new keyboard functions. For example, the ENTER, F10, TAB, INS, and DEL keys work identically to the way they work with PFS:WRITE, PFS:REPORT, and PFS:GRAPH. The function keys on the left of the keyboard can be used for special functions whenever they are displayed in the status area at the bottom of

```
        PFS:FILE FUNCTION MENU
        ------------------------


    1   DESIGN FILE         5   PRINT

    2   ADD                 6   REMOVE

    3   COPY                7   EXIT PFS:FILE

    4   SEARCH/UPDATE



        SELECTION NUMBER: 1

        FILE NAME: B:PROSPECT.DAT



    (C) 1983 Software Publishing Corporation

                                            F10-Continue
```

Figure 4-2.   PFS:FILE Main Menu

Table 4-1. *PFS:FILE Keyboard Functions*

Key	Function
F2	Prints all pages of a form
F3	Removes a record
F5	Enters current date at cursor location
F6	Enters current time at cursor location
F10	Continues or saves current record and continues
ESC	Cancels operation
TAB	Moves cursor forward between menu options or items on a form
SHIFT/TAB	Moves cursor backward between options or items on a screen
PGDN	Moves cursor down to next page of form
PGUP	Moves cursor up to preceding page of form
HOME	Moves cursor to first item on screen
CTRL/HOME	Erases current page
INS	Inserts character at cursor location
DEL	Deletes character at cursor location

the screen. Refer to Figure 1-1 if you have difficulty locating these keys. Table 4-1 lists all the keyboard functions used by **PFS:FILE**.

Before starting, be sure your **PFS:FILE** program is installed and loaded. (See Appendix C for installation instructions, if necessary.) The starting directions are the same as for starting **PFS:WRITE** (see Chapter 2) except that both the **DOS 1.0** and **DOS 2.0** operating systems can be installed on the program disk with **PFS:FILE**, so it is not necessary to switch to the **PFS:FILE** program disk after starting the computer. To begin the program, the following command is used from the system prompt:

A>**FILE** ENTER

Once the program has loaded, you will see the Main Menu of Figure 4-2. You can change a disk whenever this Main Menu is displayed. You should never change the disk at any other time using PFS:FILE because you could damage a data disk. If you have a system with a hard disk, you will not need to change disks since the data will be on the hard disk. If you are using a system with two floppy disk drives, put the disk with your data in Drive B. If you are using a single disk system, remove the PFS:FILE program disk and put your data disk in Drive A.

CREATING THE FORM

Records are stored in the computer in *files*. Each file can contain one or more records. Before storing records, you must create a form that will be used to organize the information that will be stored for each record. You can design a form almost any way you wish. You design it and then use it by filling in the blanks — just as you would fill out a paper form. If you are already using a paper form, you can create a form on the screen that looks exactly like it. You do not need to worry about running out of room for a name or a city; if the information fits on the screen in the space specified when you created the form, it will be stored correctly.

As an exercise, let us create a form that will be used to store information about prospective clients for a small business. In this example, each record (and form) will consist of only one page. Since our sample file will be used mainly for mailings, the form must include Name, Address, City, State, and ZIP Code. Let's add a Phone Number, Date, and Notes to complete it.

Now begin making the form. From the Main Menu, enter a 1 (Design File) next to "SELECTION NUMBER:", use the TAB key to move the cursor to "FILE NAME:", and enter **B:PROSPECT.DAT** as the name of the file you will create. Always use the disk drive designator, such as B:PROSPECT.DAT in Figure 4-2, to tell the computer on what drive to find or store the file. Press F10 to indicate you are ready to continue. You will see the Design File Menu of Figure 4-3. Select 1 (Create File) from this menu and press F10 to begin the design. You will then see a screen blank except for the status area at the bottom as shown in Figure 4-4. Locate all of these items in the status area:

The name of the file you are creating
The function you are using (Design)
The page of the form that is displayed
The active function keys.

Now use the CURSOR CONTROL and ENTER keys to design the form shown in Figure 4-5. Enter the title first, but do not follow it with a colon. The item name "LASTNAME" will be entered next in the upper-left corner. Always put the item that will be used to locate records most frequently in this area, since PFS:FILE can use this item to locate a record quickly. While other items can be used to locate records, it will

```
DESIGN FILE MENU


1  CREATE FILE

2  CHANGE DESIGN




SELECTION NUMBER: 1




                                       F10-Continue
```

Figure 4-3. *Design File Menu*

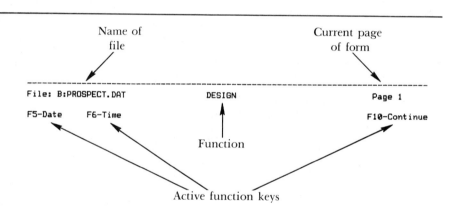

Figure 4-4. *Beginning to design the form*

take the program much longer to find the records in a large file since they will be scanned sequentially. If you want to organize the records alphabetically, put the last name in the upper-left corner. If you want to organize your records by a part number or ID number, put this number in the upper-left corner. Enter the item name you wish to use as a prompt for entry with a colon as follows:

LASTNAME:

in case you want the name first, reverse the design where applicable.

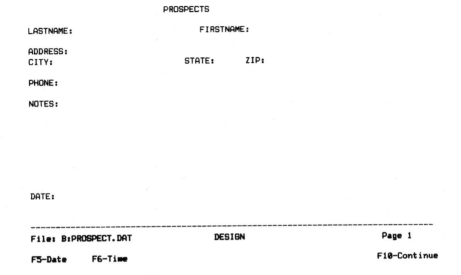

Figure 4-5. *Sample form design*

The colon indicates that the entry is an item name and not the title of the form, and that data will be entered after the item when the form is filled out. Now enter the name of the next item, **FIRSTNAME:**, on the same line as "LASTNAME:" (follow the format of Figure 4-5 as you do this). Press ENTER twice to move down two lines, and continue in this way as you put in the rest of the form. *Be very careful to use a colon after every item name.* You can use either upper- or lowercase letters, but the case will not change when the item is used for retrieval or editing. Use the CURSOR CONTROL keys to move the cursor to correct a mistake. When you have finished entering the items for this form, press F10 to return to the Main Menu. This new form will be saved and ready to receive record data.

ADDING THE RECORDS

To begin adding records to the new file, select function **2** (Add) from the Main Menu. Your file name is already displayed, so you don't have to enter it. Press F10 to continue. You will then see your blank form with the status information on the bottom of the screen as shown in Figure 4-6. Look for the following information in the status area.

The name of the file
The number of the record (form) you are adding to the file
The page of the form currently displayed
Which function keys are active.

Any highlighted areas on the form are item names and are a permanent part of the form. If your screen does not match the highlighting shown in the figure, you may have omitted a colon, which signifies item name. If you need to make corrections, reenter the Design File Menu by pressing ESC, selecting function 1 (Design File), and pressing F10. On the Design File Menu, select option 2 (Change Design) and press F10. Your form is now displayed in its current form. You can now use the CURSOR CONTROL keys to move the cursor and edit the form, adding the colon or making any necessary changes. Once the corrections are made, use F10 to store the new design and return to the Main Menu. Select function 2 (Add) and press F10 to begin adding data again.

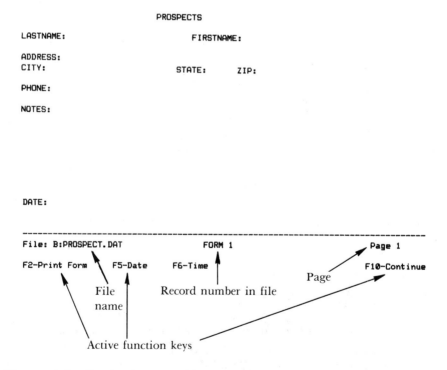

Figure 4-6. *Beginning to add a record*

```
                          PROSPECTS

        LASTNAME: CHRISTMAS           FIRSTNAME: MARY

        ADDRESS: 234 FOX ROAD
        CITY: PORTLAND              STATE: OR   ZIP: 97212

        PHONE: (503) 555-2835

        NOTES: HAS A CAT NAMED ANGEL




        DATE: 84/07/30


    ----------------------------------------------------------------------
    File: B:PROSPECT.DAT              FORM 1                    Page 1

    F2-Print Form      F5-Date     F6-Time                  F10-Continue
```

Figure 4-7. *The first record*

To create your first record, fill in the form with the information shown in Figure 4-7. Use the TAB key to move forward between items on the form and the TAB and SHIFT keys to move backward. You will notice that the TAB key always positions the cursor two characters to the right of the displayed colon to enter an item value. Try using the ENTER key to move the cursor to an item at the beginning of a line, and you will see the cursor is positioned one character from the displayed colon for an item value. To give your file consistency, avoid using ENTER to add records, and use TAB to move the cursor between items. (In searches, the extra beginning space generated by using the ENTER key is ignored, so records can be located correctly if either the TAB or ENTER key is used.) Continue to fill in the form and notice how easily and quickly information can be entered. When you get to the entry "DATE:", position the cursor using the TAB key and press F5. The current date will be entered for the item. Notice that when the date is entered using the F5 key, it is entered in yy/mm/dd order. This enables any sort on the date to work properly, as you would generally wish to sort on the year first, then the month, and finally the day.

If you make a mistake while typing in an item value, backspace and correct the value. If the mistake is on another item value, use the TAB key with the SHIFT key to move backward to the item and reenter the value. You can reenter all the values on the page by pressing CTRL and HOME. This will clear any information you have entered for that record.

Once you have entered the values for each item, press F10 and the values will be stored. The screen will then show an empty form, and the status will show you are entering item values for the second record ("FORM 2"). Enter four more records with the following names and addresses in this way.

Bestguess, Mark
12 Longwood Drive
Pittsburgh, PA 15222
(412) 555-3214

Doe, John
Box 375
Jackson, MS 39200
(601) 555-8745

Weasel, Willie
213 Lane Street
Portland, OR 97212
(503) 555-2167

Smith, Bill
Box 2013
St. Louis, MO 63100
(314) 555-2391

Press F10 after the last record. You have now stored five records and have a blank screen for the sixth record entry. Press ESC and you will return to the Main Menu.

NOTE: If you press the ESC key at any other time during the Add function with a record displayed on the screen, the values will not be saved for that particular record and you will be returned to the Main Menu.

COPYING THE FILE

Once you have designed a file and put records into it, your next step is to copy the file. This will protect your information in case something happens to the original file. Therefore, before continuing, create at least one copy of your PROSPECT file.

NOTE: The Copy function in PFS:FILE can only be used on dual drive systems or on systems with a hard disk. If you have a single drive system, you must exit the PFS:FILE program and use the COPY or DSKCOPY utilities in the operating system to copy a file.

To copy your file, select function **3** (Copy) from the Main Menu and press F10. You will then see the Copy Menu as shown in Figure 4-8. Now enter option **3** (Copy Whole File). TAB to the query for the file name, and enter a new file name for your document, such as **B:PROSPECT.BAK**. (Be sure to use a disk designator.) The file name you enter on this menu *must* be different from the file name you used on the Main Menu, because PFS:FILE will copy information *from* the file you named on the Main Menu (PROSPECT.DAT) *to* the file name

```
COPY FUNCTION MENU


1   COPY DESIGN ONLY

2   COPY SELECTED FORMS

3   COPY WHOLE FILE



SELECTION NUMBER: 3

NEW FILE NAME: B:PROSPECT.BAK




                                      F10-Continue
```

Figure 4-8.   *The Copy Menu*

you selected on the Copy Menu (PROSPECT.BAK). Press F10. PFS:FILE will now copy your original file to PROSPECT.BAK.

There is another way to copy records if you need to copy only certain records. From the Main Menu select function **3** (Copy) and press F10. When the Copy Function Menu (Figure 4-8) is displayed, select option **1** (Copy Design Only) and then enter **B:PROSPECT.BAK** next to "NEW FILE NAME:". Press F10, and read this message:

THAT FILE ALREADY EXISTS

The Copy function did not work because you must use a new file name. Try again with a new name; use **B:TEMP2.DAT**, and press F10 again. This time a new file will be created that will contain only the design of the original file. There will be no records in your new file. Select option **2** from the Copy Function Menu (Copy Selected Forms), and press F10. You will see a blank form displayed. You can now enter specifications to control *which* records are moved to the new file. (The use of specifications will be more fully discussed in Chapter 10.) Since we wish *all* the records to be copied, press F10. You will see each record displayed as it is copied to TEMP2.DAT.

DELETING A FILE

PFS:FILE does not have a function that permits you to delete an entire file. To delete a file, you must select function **7** (Exit PFS:FILE) and leave the program. You can then use the ERASE or DEL commands in DOS to delete a file. If you need help, refer to your DOS manual. PFS:FILE does have a function for removing all or specific resources from a file without removing the file or the file specification. This function will be described in Chapter 10.

RETRIEVING THE RECORDS YOU WANT

Since the backup copy of the file has been made, you can now feel safe in using your new file. The only way to use the records is to retrieve them. The Search/Update function (function 4 on the Main Menu) retrieves specific records and then displays, updates, or removes them from the file. PFS:FILE provides five methods of locating and retrieving

```
                    PROSPECTS

     LASTNAME:                  FIRSTNAME:

     ADDRESS:
     CITY:                  STATE:      ZIP: 97212

     PHONE:

     NOTES:




     DATE:


     -------------------------------------------------------------
     File: B:PROSPECT.DAT          RETRIEVE SPEC           Page 1

     F5-Date     F6-Time                              F10-Continue
```

Figure 4-9. *Specifying the selection criteria*

records. For now, we will examine only the full item match. In Chapter 10 we will examine the other four methods.

To search your file, press ESC. From the Main Menu, select function 4 (Search/Update) and enter your file name, **B:PROSPECT.DAT**. Press F10 and you will see an empty form with the words "RETRIEVE SPEC" at the bottom of the screen as shown in Figure 4-9. Use this form to select *which* records you want to retrieve. TAB to the "ZIP:" item and enter **97212**. Press F10, and the program will begin to search the file for an address in which the ZIP item matches the code you entered. When the program finds a record, the search will stop and the entire record will be displayed. At this point you can just view the entire record or TAB to any item you wish to change and type over the current value, or delete the whole record by pressing the F3 key. If you decide not to change the record, you can press the ESC key and the update or deletion will not be saved. If you press F10, the action will be completed, the record will be changed or deleted, and the next form that matches the search criteria will be displayed.

Remember, use F10 to move through the file, display each match, and view, edit, or delete an entry. Use ESC at any time to abort the scan and return to the Main Menu. The records will be displayed in the opposite order from the order in which you entered them; that is, the last record you entered will be retrieved first.

. When you complete the scan, you will see a screen that shows how many records (forms) PFS:FILE found that matched your search criteria:

Forms found: 2

Press F10 to continue

Pressing F10 will return you to the Main Menu. Once again, *never* remove a disk containing data from your computer while running PFS:FILE unless the Main Menu is displayed. If you remove a disk at any other time, you will destroy information that you have written to the disk.

PRINTING THE RECORDS

After you have created a file, you can print the records it contains. For example, suppose you wish to print mailing labels for the addresses you have just stored. (You can also print addresses to Rolodex stock, which can be purchased in a continuous form.) To print the addresses, select function **5** (Print) from the Main Menu and press F10. This will begin the process of printing. Before the labels can be printed, however, you must do three things:

1. Select which records to print.

2. Select print options: whether the item names will be printed, the number of lines per page, and the number of copies to print.

3. Enter the print specifications: the order in which the items should be printed and how they will appear on the page.

In the first step, we are selecting the *records* that are to be printed. In the third step, we are selecting the *items* in these records to print.

When the print function begins, the screen will display a blank form (see Figure 4-10). "RETRIEVE SPEC" appears at the bottom of the screen since this form is used to select *which* records from your file to print. Later, in Chapter 10, you will see how to select specific records for

```
                         PROSPECTS

    LASTNAME:                    FIRSTNAME:

    ADDRESS:
    CITY:                    STATE:     ZIP:

    PHONE:

    NOTES:




    DATE:

    ------------------------------------------------------------------------
    File: B:PROSPECT.DAT           RETRIEVE SPEC           Page 1

    F5-Date     F6-Time                                  F10-Continue
```

Figure 4-10.   Specifying the records to be printed

printing. For now, let's print *all* of the records in the file. Press F10. This will select all records.

The next screen displayed is used to select the print options (see Figure 4-11). Since we are printing mailing labels, we do not wish to print the names of the items with the item values on the printout. Enter **N** next to the "PRINT ITEM NAMES (Y/N):". Next to the "PRINT TO:" enter your printer port type. Enter **LPT1:** if you are using a parallel printer. If you are using a serial printer, see Appendix C for details.

To enter the correct response to "LINES PER PAGE:", you will need to know the number of lines on your mailing label between the top of one label to the top of the next label. Measure this for your labels and enter it. ("7" has been used in this example.) Enter 1 for the number of copies, and press F10 to continue to the next screen.

This third screen is used to enter the print specifications and determines which items will be printed, where they will be printed, and the order in which the records will be printed. In this example, we will print the Lastname, Firstname, Address, City, State, and ZIP code. These are the only items for which you will enter information on this form. The other items should be left blank. Complete the form as

```
                    PRINT OPTIONS


            PRINT ITEM NAMES (Y/N): N

            PRINT TO: LPT1:

            LINES PER PAGE: 7

            NUMBER OF COPIES: 1




                                        F10-Continue
```

Figure 4-11.   *Selecting the print options*

shown in Figure 4-12. Enter an **X** next to "FIRSTNAME:" and
"ADDRESS:". This will cause the printer to print the value and move
to the beginning of the next line. Enter + next to "LASTNAME:",
"CITY:", and "STATE:". This causes the item value to print two spaces
to the right of the previously printed item. Enter **SX** next to "ZIP:".
This causes the labels to be printed in ZIP code order and moves the
printer to the beginning of a new line after printing each ZIP code. In
summary, the print specification options are as follows:

X   Prints the value, and advances printer to the next line.

+   Prints the value two spaces to the right of the last item printed.

S   Indicates the item according to which output is to be sorted. The
    "S" can be combined with other values when entered first.

Once you have entered the print specification values, press F10 to
initiate printing. Try to print your labels now on regular paper to see
how the labels print and check the spacing. Since **PFS:FILE** uses an
almost free-form entry for item values, it is possible to create a long
name or address line that will not fit on your label. Be sure to check this
during entry or after printing so that labels print properly.

```
                    PROSPECTS

LASTNAME: +                    FIRSTNAME: X


ADDRESS: X
CITY: +                   STATE: +   ZIP: SX

PHONE:

NOTES:




DATE:

----------------------------------------------------------------------
File: B:PROSPECT.DAT          PRINT SPEC              Page 1

F5-Date    F6-Time                                   F10-Continue
```

Figure 4-12.   *Print specifications*

```
                         BESTGUESS  MARK
                         12 LONGWODD DRIVE
                         PITTSBURGH  PA  15222




                         DOE  JOHN
                         BOX 375
                         JACKSON  MS  39200




                         SMITH  BILL
                         BOX 2013
                         ST. LOUIS  MO  63100




                         WEASEL  WILLIE
                         213 LANE STREET
                         PORTLAND  OR  97212




                         CHRISTMAS  MARY
                         234 FOX ROAD
                         PORTLAND  OR  97212
```

Figure 4-13.   *The printed output*

The printed output is shown in Figure 4-13. After the printer completes the printing, you will see the message screen

Forms printed: 5

Press F10 to continue

Press F10 to return to the Main Menu. You now have the data saved in two files: B:PROSPECT.DAT and B:PROSPECT.BAK.

LEAVING PFS:FILE

When you have finished creating and editing your files, select function **7** (Exit PFS:FILE) from the Main Menu. This will return you to your computer's operating system and you will see the operating system prompt:

A>

From this prompt, you can enter the name of any other program you wish to use.

CHAPTER
FIVE

Using PFS:REPORT

PFS:REPORT is a report generator that can be used with PFS:FILE to print tabular reports. PFS:REPORT expands the reporting capabilities of PFS:FILE in the following ways:

- Reports can be printed in tabular form with as many as 16 columns defined.

- Report specifications can be pre-defined or saved and used repeatedly.

- Mathematical operations like the creation of totals, subtotals, averages, or subaverages can be assigned to report columns.

- Counts and subcounts can be performed.

- A column can be printed in which the values are derived from other columns; for example, the extended cost of inventory items can be calculated from the item cost times the quantity of each item on hand.

The first two capabilities are described in this chapter; the remaining three in Chapter 11, "Integrating PFS Software."

Like PFS:WRITE and PFS:FILE, PFS:REPORT is easy to learn and use. You will find that commands you have already learned in PFS:WRITE and PFS:FILE apply as well to PFS:REPORT. Many of the steps you have learned in PFS:FILE to locate records and to control the files work identically in PFS:REPORT. You need only learn the new features. You will learn some of these new features in this chapter and the more complex ones in Chapter 11. Be sure you understand how to use PFS:FILE before trying to learn PFS:REPORT.

INTRODUCING PFS:REPORT

PFS:REPORT is specifically designed to print tabular reports and is not directly applicable to other types of record printing such as mailing labels. For nontabular reports, use PFS:FILE. You cannot use PFS:REPORT with any other type of input data than that from PFS:FILE. You use many of the features of PFS:REPORT in the same way you used them in PFS:FILE. The functions and options you use are selected from menus. As with PFS:FILE, there are three basic steps to creating the report:

1. Selecting which records from the file you wish to print.

2. Selecting the report options (title, lines per page, and page width).

3. Entering the report specifications (which items of the record to print, what column should be used for each item, and how the records should be sorted).

In the first step you are selecting which *records* to print. In the last step you are selecting which *items* in these records to print. Report specifications (which items to print, the columns to use, and how the records should be sorted) can be saved and used again. Setting up the selection criteria for the records you want from the file (step 1) and sorting these (done by PFS:REPORT after step 3) must be done each time you print a report.

How the function keys work in PFS:REPORT is almost identical to how they work in PFS:FILE. Table 5-1 presents a summary of the keyboard functions.

Table 5-1. *PFS:REPORT Keyboard Functions*

F3	Remove report specifications
F7	Set up a derived columns screen
F10	Continue
ESC	Cancel operation
TAB	Move cursor forward between menu options or items on a form
SHIFT/TAB	Move cursor backward between options or items on a screen
PGDN	Move cursor down to next page of form
PGUP	Move cursor up to preceding page of form
HOME	Move cursor to first item on screen
CTRL/HOME	Erase current page
INS	Insert character at cursor location
DEL	Delete character at cursor location

MAKING A FILE

Before you can print a report, you must, of course, have already created a data file with PFS:FILE. You will use PFS:FILE to create a new file and then use PFS:REPORT to design a report that will be used with the file.

Suppose you are a manufacturer of modem products. (A *modem* is a device that enables a computer to communicate by telephone lines with other computers.) You wish to create a file of all your competitors, identifying each manufacturer and each of its modem products. For purposes of this exercise, you need not create a complete file, just enter six or more entries that will show how the program works. (On the other hand, you may wish to enter a dozen or more to gain a better insight into the reporting capabilities.) The example file could be applied to almost any manufacturing application.

Table 5-2 shows the data that you will be entering using PFS:FILE. Using PFS:FILE, create a form for your records like the one shown in Figure 5-1. Name this form **B:MODEMS.DAT** and enter the data for six or more of the modem products from Table 5-2. Refer back to Chapter 4 if you need help in creating this file. Don't worry if some of the terms in the data are unfamiliar. If you prefer, you may use a product with which

Table 5-2. Input Data for the Exercise

MODEM PRODUCTS

MANUFACTURER	MODEL	COMPUTER INTERFACE	TELEPHONE INTERFACE	SPEED	NOTES
ANCHOR AUTOMATION	MARK 1	RS-232-C	DIRECT	110-300	HAYES COMPATIBLE
	MARK 12	RS-232-C	DIRECT	300-1200	
	MARK II	ATARI 850	DIRECT	110-300	
	MARK III	RS-232-C	DIRECT	300/1200	
ANDERSON JACOBSON, INC.	A242A	RS-232-C	ACOUSTIC	100-300+	
BIZCOMP CORPORATION	1080	VIC,APPLE	DIRECT	300	SWITCHES BOTH VOICE AND DATA, INCLUDES SOFTWARE
	PC:INTELLIMODEM	RS-232-C	DIRECT	300/1200	
HAYES MICROCOMPUTER PRODUCTS	1200b	IBM PC/XT	DIRECT	110-1200	PLUG-IN BOARD WITH AUTO-DIAL, MONITOR, SOFTWARE
	SMARTMODEM 1200	RS-232-C	DIRECT	110-1200	AUTO-DIAL, MONITOR
	SMARTMODEM 300	RS-232-C	DIRECT	110/300+	AUTO-DIAL, MONITOR
MFJ ENTERPRISES	MFJ-1232	APPLE+	ACOUSTIC	110/300	OPTIONAL SOFTWARE
MICROPERIPHERAL CORPORATION	MICROMATION A1	ATARI 850	DIRECT	300	OPTIONAL AUTO-DIAL, AUTO-ANSWER
	MICROMATION O1	OSBORNE-1	DIRECT	300	
NOVATION	212 APPLE CAT II	APPLE	DIRECT	110-1200	APPLE NOVATION CARD UPGRADE FOR 1200 BAUD
	APPLE CAT II	APPLE	DIRECT	300-1200	AUTO-DIAL, REDIAL
PRENTICE CORPORATION	POPCOM X100	RS-232-C	DIRECT	300/1200	AUTO-DIAL
TANDY CORPORATION	DC-1200	RS-232-C	DIRECT	300/1200	AUTO-DIAL OPTIONAL
VEN-TEL, INC.	PC MODEM PLUS	IBM PC/XT	DIRECT	110-1200	HAYES COMPATIBLE, INCLUDES CROSSTALK SOFTWARE

```
                    MODEM PRODUCTS

COMPANY:

MODEL:


COMPUTER INTERFACE:
TELEPHONE INTERFACE:
SPEED:


NOTES:




LAST UPDATE:

-----------------------------------------------------------------
File: B:MODEMS.DAT              DESIGN                    Page 1

F5-Date      F6-Time                                F10-Continue
```

Figure 5-1. *Modem product form*

you are familiar and define the items to match your needs. When entering records to your file, be sure to include at least one example with two or more products for one company.

Once you have entered your records, use PFS:FILE to look them over and correct any mistakes you have made. When the entries have been corrected, you are ready to try PFS:REPORT. Be sure to create a copy of **B:MODEMS.DAT** before leaving PFS:FILE.

Entering the Retrieval Specifications

The first step in the printing of a report is starting PFS:REPORT and entering the retrieval specifications. This determines *which* of the records to print. As with **PFS:WRITE** and **PFS:FILE**, **PFS:REPORT** should already be properly installed for your computer system. If this is not true, refer to Appendix C for appropriate installation instructions. You should also have already used PFS:FILE (Chapter 4) and gained some proficiency in the creation of files.

The starting directions are similar to those for starting PFS:WRITE

```
PFS:  R E P O R T
------------------

1  PRINT A REPORT

2  PRE-DEFINE A REPORT

3  SET NEW HEADINGS

4  EXIT PFS:REPORT


SELECTION NUMBER: 1

FILE NAME: B:MODEMS.DAT



       (C) 1983 Software Publishing Corporation
                                                F10-continue
```

Figure 5-2. Main Menu

(see Chapter 2) except that the DOS operating system (whether version 1 or 2) can be installed on the PFS:REPORT program disk, so it is not necessary to switch from the DOS disk to the PFS:REPORT program disk after starting the computer. When you have the system prompt, you load the program by entering the following command:

A>**REPORT** ENTER

Once the program has been loaded, you will see the Main Menu, shown in Figure 5-2. If you need to change a disk, you can do so whenever this Main Menu is displayed. You should never change the disk at any other time when using PFS:REPORT, because doing so could damage a data disk. (If you have a hard disk system, you should not need to change disks, as the data will be on the hard disk.) If you are using a system with two disk drives, you put the data disk in Drive B. If you are using a single disk system, remove the PFS:REPORT program disk and put in your data disk.

Choosing the Records

Once all disks are in place and PFS:REPORT has been loaded, select item 1 (Print a Report) from the Main Menu. Use the TAB key to move the cursor to "FILE NAME:" and enter the file name you used to create the file — **B:MODEMS.DAT**. Use the "B:" as a part of the name if you have two disk drives. Press F10. You should then see a form that is the same as Figure 5-1 except that the status line reads RETRIEVE SPEC instead of DESIGN. In this form you enter your retrieval specifications. Specific records can be retrieved using this form much as they were in using PFS:FILE. (In Chapter 9 you will learn how to do more complex retrievals that are useful when you don't want to print all of the records.) Since here you want to print all of the records, press F10 again and the Report Options Menu is displayed.

Choosing the Report Options

You can select your report options from the Report Options Menu now displayed (see Figure 5-3). These options can be defined as follows:

TITLE: Defines the title of the report that will be printed on every page. It cannot be more than one line.

PRE-DEFINED REPORT NAME: Permits you to print a report from a report specification you created earlier for another report and saved.

OUTPUT TO: Permits you to select where the output of the report will be directed. Normally, you will direct it to a parallel printer (LPT1:) or serial printer (COM1: or AUX:). You can also direct the

```
                    REPORT OPTIONS



        TITLE: MODEM PRODUCTS

        PRE-DEFINED REPORT NAME:



        OUTPUT TO: lpt1:

        LINES PER PAGE: 66        PAGE WIDTH: 80
```

Figure 5-3.   *Setting the report options*

report to a disk file by giving a file name such as B:MODEMS.PRN. (Any extension will work, so it is advisable to use a consistent one such as PRN for all output printing.) You can then use this file with PFS:WRITE to put the report in a document. LPT1: is the default assignment as shown in Figure 5-3. This option is discussed in more depth in Chapter 11.

LINES PER PAGE: The number of lines on each sheet of paper. The number normally is 66, but you may wish to change this for labels or special forms. Top and bottom margins are automatically calculated.

PAGE WIDTH: The width of your paper measured in characters. Standard size paper (8 1/2 × 11-inch paper) is 80 characters wide. If you are using extra-wide paper, you can change this character count accordingly. Also, if you are using compressed print (17 characters per inch) or 12 characters per inch, you will need to change this setting *and* use the printer program on your PFS:REPORT disk to send the necessary codes to the printer to set it up. You can use any value from 40 to 255 characters total (see Appendix C).

For this example, the only report option you will need to enter is the report title. Enter **MODEM PRODUCTS** next to "TITLE:", leave the rest of the items at their default values, and press F10. A blank form is now displayed on the screen.

Entering the Report Specifications

The final step before printing is entering the report specifications. You enter these on the blank form now displayed entitled MODEM PROD-UCTS (see Figure 5-4). During this step, you will identify which items are to be printed by assigning each a column number and defining what is to be printed in each column. An item is printed only if it has been given a column number. The report can contain as many as 16 columns, with the leftmost column being number 1.

PFS:REPORT automatically sorts the information into alphabetic or numeric order using both columns 1 and 2. For this reason, whatever you select to print in column 1 will determine the primary order of the report. Items with the same values for column 1 are listed in order by column 2. If the report contains more than one record with the same

```
                    MODEM PRODUCTS

     COMPANY: 1

     MODEL: 2


     COMPUTER INTERFACE: 3
     TELEPHONE INTERFACE:
     SPEED:


     NOTES:




     LAST UPDATE:
     -----------------------------------------------------------------------
     File: B:MODEMS.DAT           REPORT SPEC                    Page 1

     F7-Derived Columns                                       F10-continue
```

Figure 5-4. *Entering the report specification*

column 1 value, the records will be further sorted on the basis of what is selected for column 2. In the exercise, you will want to list the products first by manufacturer and then by model, so select the company name for column 1 and model type for column 2. If you print a report that you do not wish to sort in any order, define the first column as column 3. Eliminating the sort will save time, particularly on long reports.

If you wanted to use a price or any column with a numeric value, you would use an "N" with the column number in the report specifications, such as "5N". This would force the printing of the price in column 5 as a numeric value, with decimal points aligned. All numeric values are always stored as character strings in the file. The N is necessary to enable PFS:REPORT to interpret the data for this column as numeric and to align the numbers by decimal point or by the last digit.

PRINTING THE REPORT

When you have finished entering the report specifications, turn the printer on and press F10. The report will begin to print. As the report is printed, notice that the screen will show the records being sorted and then display each record as it is printed. Figure 5-5 shows what your report would look like if you made a record for each modem in Table

```
                              MODEM PRODUCTS

          MODEM PRODUCTS              PART           COMPUTER INTERFACE
     -------------------------    -----------------  ------------------
     ANCHOR AUTOMATION            MARK 1             RS-232-C
                                  MARK 12            RS-232-C
                                  MARK II            ATARI 850
                                  MARK III           RS-232-C

     ANDERSON JACOBSON, INC       A242A              RS-232-C
     BIZCOMP CORPORATION          1080               VIC, APPLE
                                  PC:INTELLIMODEM    RS-232-C

     HAYES MICROCOMPUTER PRODUCTS 1200b              IBM PC/XT
                                  SMARTMODEM 1200    RS-232-C
                                  SMARTMODEM 300     RS-232-C

     MFJ ENTERPRISES              MFJ-1232           APPLE+
     MICROPERIPHERAL CORPORATION  MICROMATION A1     ATARI 850
                                  MICROMATION O1     OSBORNE-1

     NOVATION                     212 APPLE CAT II   APPLE
                                  APPLE CAT II       APPLE

     PRENTICE CORPORATION         POPCOM X100        RS-232-C
     TANDY CORPORATION            DC-1200            RS-232-C
     VEN-TEL, INC.                PC MODEM PLUS      IBM PC/XT
```

Figure 5-5.   The report

5-2. The width of each printed column is automatically determined by the length of the column heading *and* the length of the longest item value in the column that will print. PFS:REPORT must scan all of the records before it can determine how to create the columns. Notice also that the modem manufacturer (column 1) is printed only once for each group of products for that manufacturer. The table is in alphabetical order by manufacturer name, with the products in alphanumeric order for each manufacturer. After each group of products by a single manufacturer, a line is automatically skipped.

If you have a wide printer and can set the printer to twelve characters per inch, print the report shown in Table 5-2. In most cases, you will need to set the printer to twelve characters per inch either using a separate program (a BASIC program, for instance) or using Appendix C and installing PFS:REPORT for twelve characters per inch. In this case, when you start to print with PFS:REPORT, select 160 characters as the page width on the Report Options screen. When you create the record, use the report specifications displayed in Figure 5-6.

PFS:REPORT is able to format reports in which columns must be calculated or totals determined. In Chapter 11 you will see how.

```
                    MODEM PRODUCTS

   COMPANY: 1

   MODEL: 2



   COMPUTER INTERFACE: 3
   TELEPHONE INTERFACE: 4
   SPEED: 5


   NOTES: 6




   LAST UPDATE:

   -------------------------------------------------------------------------
   File: B:MODEMS.DAT            REPORT SPEC              Page 1

   F7-Derived Columns                                    F10-continue
```

Figure 5-6.   *Report retrieval specifications*

PRE-DEFINING REPORT SPECIFICATIONS

If you need to print the same report several times or periodically, you can enter the report specifications once and save them with a name using the Pre-defined Reports function. You will still need to enter the retrieval specification each time, but you will save the bother of entering the report specifications.

To save the report specifications, select function **2** (Pre-define a Report) from the Main Menu. After pressing F10 you will see the screen shown in Figure 5-7. Next to "REPORT NAME:" enter a name that will be descriptive of your report. Enter **MODEMS**.

NOTE: When saving report specifications, do *not* use a disk designator or extension. The specifications are saved as part of your data file (MODEMS.DAT) and *not* as a separate file. This arrangement keeps a user from inadvertently assigning the wrong specifications to a file.

PRE-DEFINED REPORTS:

(None)

REPORT NAME: MODEMS

F10-continue

Figure 5-7. *Saving a report specification*

Once you have entered the file name, press F10, and you will again see the form that you constructed earlier (see Figure 5-1). As you did before, enter the column numbers for the items you wish to print (see Figure 5-4). Press F10. The specifications are now saved, and the Main Menu is on the screen.

Now see if the specifications were saved. Select function 1 (Print a Report) from the Main Menu and press F10 again to select all records in the file for printing. When the Report Options Menu is displayed, enter the report title **MODEM PRODUCTS** and the file name for the pre-defined specification:

PRE-DEFINED REPORT NAME: **MODEMS**

Turn the printer on, press F10, and the report will print.

Changing Column Headings

So far, the column headings in the printed reports have been the same as the item names you typed in to make the product form (Figure 5-1). There may be occasions when you wish to change the column headings

```
                            MODEM PRODUCTS

        COMPANY:

        MODEL:


        COMPUTER INTERFACE: INTERFACE
        TELEPHONE INTERFACE:
        SPEED:


        NOTES:




        LAST UPDATE:
        ------------------------------------------------------------------------
        File: B:MODEMS.DAT              HEADINGS                     Page 1

        F3-Remove                                               F10-continue
```

Figure 5-8. *Changing the headings*

before printing the report. To change the headings, return to the Main
Menu if it is not displayed (do so by pressing ESC) and select function 3
(Set New Headings). Enter the name of the file you will use for the data
input—in this case, **B:MODEMS.DAT**—and press F10. You will then
see a form displaying the record items as in Figure 5-1. Use the TAB key
to move the cursor to any item for which you wish to change the heading, and next to it enter the new heading name for that item (see Figure
5-8). If you do not enter a new heading for an item, the original item
name will continue to be used for a heading. When you have finished,
press F10. The headings will be saved and used in all subsequent reports
from that file until you change them again. Print the revised report. In
changing headings, remember that the length of the headings and the
length of the data jointly determine how wide PFS:REPORT will make
each column. Be sure you have enough space on your page for the new
headings. If you ever wish to remove all of the headings you have
entered and revert to the item names for column headings, select function 3 (Set New Headings) from the Main Menu and press F10. When
the headings are displayed, press F3 and all of the alternate headings
will be deleted and the headings will revert to the item names. Note that
this technique restores *all* changed headings.

LEAVING PFS:REPORT

When you have finished printing the last report, select function 4 from the Main Menu. This will return you to your computer's operating system and you will see the prompt:

A>

From this prompt, you can enter the name of any other program you wish to use.

CHAPTER
SIX

Using PFS:GRAPH

Charts and graphs can help busy people analyze data quickly because they visually summarize the words and numbers presented in reports. In general, graphs illustrate the relationship between two or more sets of data. PFS:GRAPH creates graphs using a dot matrix printer or a plotter from data in files created by PFS:FILE, from DIF files created by certain spreadsheet programs like VisiCalc or Lotus 1-2-3, or from data entered manually to the PFS:GRAPH program.

You can create three types of graphs with PFS:GRAPH: the line graph, the bar graph, and the pie graph (see Figure 6-1). Selecting which type of graph to use will depend on what you want to communicate. Bar graphs are best used to illustrate quantitative information; in particular, to show comparisons between groups of data. For example, a bar graph could show the sales volumes of several products made by a single manufacturer. Line graphs, in contrast, are best used to show trends or changes in data over time; for example, the actual or projected sales of a product over a specified period of time. The pie graph compares parts in relationship to the whole by showing data in percentages.

In PFS:GRAPH, a chart is composed of one to four graphs. A special type of line chart, called an *area chart*, is used to show the relative

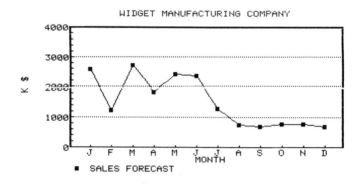

LINE

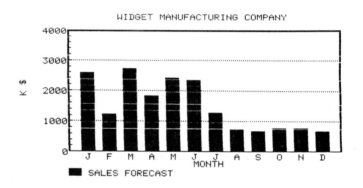

BAR

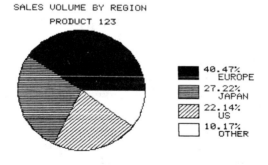

PIE

Figure 6-1. *Three types of graphs*

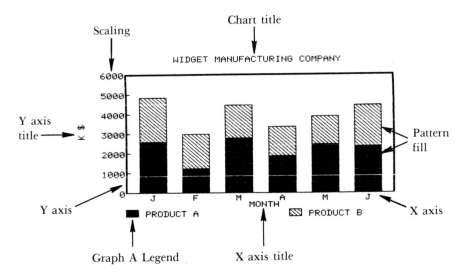

Figure 6-2. *The chart components*

importance of different items, such as comparing the sales of several items over a period of time. In this case you would have two or more line graphs.

Bar and line graphs use horizontal and vertical axes for their basic format. The horizontal row is called the *X axis,* and the vertical line is called the *Y axis.* The X axis shows data classification or time; for example, the month or age. The Y axis shows the quantitative value. For example, the bar graph in Figure 6-2 shows time (MONTH) along the X axis and amount (K $) along the Y axis.

PFS:GRAPH includes several special features — automatic formatting, scaling, legend labeling, and pattern fill (see Figure 6-2). Data can be compared by mixing line and bar graphs, or bar graphs can be stacked and compared side by side. As many as four graphs can be put on a single horizontal axis. If you have a color plotter, you can produce color graphs. The printed graphs can be copied and used as transparencies in presentations. Charts can also be quickly integrated with reports and documents created with PFS:WRITE.

PFS:GRAPH can create two types of disk files. The chart image can be saved as a "picture" file and used as input to other programs like PFS:WRITE. (This is *not* a standard ASCII file and is not intended to be used as input to spreadsheet or database management programs.) In addition, all of the information used to create the graph (headers, coordinate ranges, type of graph, and data) can be saved to the disk as a "chart" file and can be used by PFS:GRAPH to recreate the graph without using the initial data file again.

The hardware requirements of PFS:GRAPH are more extensive than those of other PFS programs and are described in Appendix B. In summary, the selection of printers is more limited and, with the IBM PC, a Color/Graphics Adapter Card and Color Monitor are required. You may also wish to use a plotter to produce higher-quality graphs.

In doing the exercises in this chapter, you may find an error code displayed on your screen. You may have done something wrong, or perhaps you got too adventurous and tried something that was beyond the scope of the exercise. If an error code is displayed, check your PFS:GRAPH manual. The messages are all listed in alphabetical order. Look up the message you found displayed, and the appendix will tell you what happened and how to correct it.

STARTING PFS:GRAPH

Like the other Software Publishing programs, each key serves a specific function (see Figure 1-1). The F10 key is used in much the same way as the ENTER key in other (non-PFS) programs, and the TAB key is used to move between selections on a menu. The key functions for PFS:GRAPH are presented in Table 6-1.

Table 6-1. *PFS:GRAPH Keyboard Functions*

Key	Function
F10	Continue or save current resource and continue
ESC	Cancel operation
TAB	Move cursor forward between menu options
SHIFT/TAB	Move curor backward between options on a menu
PGDN	Move cursor down to next page of form
PGUP	Move cursor up to preceding page of form
HOME	Move cursor to first item on screen
CTRL/HOME	Erase current page
INS	Insert character at cursor location
DEL	Delete character at cursor location

```
PFS:GRAPH MAIN MENU
--------------------


    1   GET/EDIT DATA        5   PRINT CHART

    2   DEFINE CHART         6   PLOT CHART

    3   DISPLAY CHART        7   CLEAR CHART

    4   GET/SAVE/REMOVE      8   EXIT PFS:GRAPH




           SELECTION NUMBER:
```

Figure 6-3. *Main Menu*

If PFS:GRAPH has not already been installed for your computer and printer, refer to Appendix C for installation instructions.

The operating system cannot be installed on the program disk with the program, so it is necessary to switch to the program disk after starting your system. To begin loading PFS:GRAPH, place the program disk in Drive A. Type the following command after the system prompt is displayed:

A>**GRAPH** ENTER

Once the program has loaded, you should see the Main Menu shown in Figure 6-3. You can change a disk whenever this Main Menu is displayed. You should never change the disk at any other time using PFS:GRAPH, as this could damage a data disk. If you have a system with a hard disk, you should not need to change disks, as the data will be on the hard disk. If you are using a system with two disk drives, you should put the data disk in Drive B. If you are using a single disk system, remove the PFS:GRAPH program disk and put your data disk in Drive A.

Four basic steps are required to create a chart with PFS:GRAPH:

1. Getting or creating the data that is to be graphed.
2. Defining the chart.
3. Printing, plotting, or displaying the chart.
4. Saving the chart.

GETTING AND EDITING THE DATA

The first step in creating a graph is to define the data to be plotted. From the Main Menu, enter **1** (Get/Edit Data) and press F10 to view the Get/Edit Data Menu shown in Figure 6-4. The menu options are as follows:

SELECTION NUMBER   Select the source of your data

1. Manual data entry (Enter/Edit Data)

2. A VisiCalc or 1-2-3 File (Get VisiCalc File)

3. A PFS:FILE (Get PFS File).

GRAPH (A/B/C/D)   Enter the graph (A,B,C,D) to which you wish to direct the data.

MERGE (Y/N)   Merges data from a second source with data that has already been loaded. The default value is "N".

DIRECTORY OR FILE NAME   Enter the complete file name if you are using a PFS:FILE, VisiCalc, or a Lotus 1-2-3 file. Leave the option blank if you wish to enter data manually. The default value is blank (manual data entry).

```
        GET/EDIT DATA MENU


    1   ENTER/EDIT DATA

    2   GET VISICALC FILE

    3   GET PFS FILE

      SELECTION NUMBER:

      GRAPH (A/B/C/D):

      MERGE (Y/N): N

      DIRECTORY OR FILE NAME:




                                      F10-Continue
```

Figure 6-4.   *The Get/Edit Menu*

X DATA FORMAT:

        X DATA   Y DATA

GRAPH A   ENTER/EDIT DATA   PAGE 1
F10-Continue

Figure 6-5. *The input data screen*

The cursor should appear after the prompt for "SELECTION NUMBER:". For this example, enter **1** (Enter/Edit Data), type **A** next to "GRAPH (A/B/C/D) ", leave the next two options at their default values ("N" and blank), and press F10 to continue. You should see the screen for input data that is shown in Figure 6-5.

The screen now shows two columns that are used to input the data to be graphed. In the top left you will see the prompt "DATA FORMAT:". This queries you for the code representing the type of data you will enter on the X axis. Three types of data can be used: identifier, numeric, and date. Identifier data is a string of characters that represent things like department names or products. Numeric data is simply numbers, and date is calendar date. For example:

Example	Type	Code
John Silver	Identifier	I
1429	Numeric	N
12/83	Date	Y, D, Q, MY, or QY

Dates can be used in a variety of formats. To represent dates on the X axis, these additional codes can be used:

Code	Type	Example
Y	Year	1984 or 84
D	Day	23
Q	Quarter	2
MY	Month/Year Format	12/84 or 12 1984 or 12 84
QY	Quarter/Year	3/84 or 3 84 or 3:84

The MY and QY formats can also be reversed to a YM or YQ format. If you use an identifier code (I) for the X axis, 1 to 15 characters are allowed for each X data item. The numeric code (N) can be used on the X axis only for line graphs.

The data for the Y axis is always considered numeric, and it is not necessary to specify any data type for the Y axis.

In the example, you wish to show sales by month. Enter an **M** to indicate months. Now TAB to the column for the X data and begin to enter your data in X,Y pairs (the data *must* be entered in pairs). The data for the X axis does not need to be entered in month order; months can be entered as numeric values. Enter the number for the first month, and then use the TAB key to move the cursor to the column to enter the first amount. Continue in this way until all the data is entered.

X DATA	Y DATA
2	1252.30
4	1843.45
1	2576.60
3	2742.85
5	2420.37
8	758.15
6	2343.25
7	1290.10
9	693.50
10	776.55
11	788.75
12	703.57

Once you have completed the data entry as shown, press F10 to return to the Main Menu again. Once you have selected the appropriate code for the X DATA FORMAT, it cannot be changed without erasing all the data you have already entered using selection 7 (Clear Chart) on the Main Menu. When the chart is cleared, you can change the data code. You must then reenter your data. You can use CTRL/HOME to clear the data, but this will not permit you to alter the data code.

DEFINING THE CHART

Your next step is to define the chart that you will use to display the data. From the Main Menu, select function **2** (Define Chart) and press F10.

```
                              DEFINE CHART MENU


                   TYPE                         LEGEND              CUM
           GRAPH
  *          A      BAR                   GRAPH A                    N
             B                            GRAPH B                    N
             C                            GRAPH C                    N
             D                            GRAPH D                    N


      CHART  TITLE:
      X-AXIS TITLE:
      Y-AXIS TITLE:


      STACK  (Y/N): N                     Y MIN:
      GRID   (Y/N): Y                     Y MAX:
      COLOR  (Y/N): N                     Y DIV:



                                                        F10-Continue
```

Figure 6-6. *The Define Chart Menu with default options*

You will then see the Define Chart Menu displayed as shown in Figure 6-6. Before you begin to define your chart, locate the following options on your screen so that you will understand the Define Chart Menu better:

* Indicates you have already entered data for the graph (A-D) it is next to. You do not enter this—it is a message from the program.

TYPE   Selects the type of graph you wish printed or displayed. Enter BAR for bar graph, LINE for line graph, or PIE for pie graph.

LEGEND   Specifies the title that will be applied to each graph. Legends can be as long as 18 characters.

CUM   Indicates whether the Y values will be accumulated for each X value before being displayed or if they will be displayed as actual values. "N" is the default value; "Y" indicates the values will be accumulated.

CHART TITLE   Allows you to enter titles for the the X axis and Y axis. These will be applied to all graphs displayed or printed on the chart.

STACK (Y/N)   Indicates whether graphs are to be displayed individually or whether the data will be combined in a single graph. Enter "N" if you wish to show each graph individually. Enter "Y" if you wish to add the Y values of the composite graphs before displaying. The default value is "N".

GRID (Y/N)   Indicates whether or not you wish to display horizontal grid lines. The default value is "Y".

COLOR (Y/N)   Indicates whether the separate graphs are to be displayed in separate colors (as with a color monitor) or in shaded colors (which is useful on some monitors like the Compaq). Enter "Y" to display the chart in color and "N" to display the chart in monochrome with shading patterns to distinguish the individual graphs (see Figure 6-2). The colors, shading, and patterns are created automatically and cannot be selected. If you select color, it will only apply to the displayed and plotted output and not to the graph printed by a dot matrix printer. The default value is "N".

Y MIN, Y MAX, Y DIV   These values can be used to adjust the scaling of the Y axis manually . The scale is a line marked on a graph to indicate proportion. Using this option, you can define your own scaling and can zoom in on a part of the graph you wish to examine closely (much like using a camera with a zoom lens). For most applications, PFS:GRAPH does an excellent job of defining the scaling automatically and these values can be left blank. You can use this option to specify the minimum or maximum value for the Y axis and to control the values for the divisions (the tick marks on the Y axis) for the coordinates.

Later in the chapter you will get a chance to try exercises with the CUM, STACK, and GRID options.

For the example, enter **BAR** under "TYPE" next to Graph "A", then TAB to the "LEGEND" column and overtype "GRAPH A" with **SALES FORECAST**. Leave CUM at the default value of "N" and TAB past all of the entries for the other graphs (for which no data is entered) to the

```
                            DEFINE CHART MENU

                    TYPE                        LEGEND           CUM
         GRAPH
    *      A        BAR                    SALES FORECAST         N
           B                               GRAPH B               N
           C                               GRAPH C               N
           D                               GRAPH D               N


    CHART   TITLE: WIDGET MANUFACTURING SALES
    X-AXIS TITLE: MONTH
    Y-AXIS TITLE: $


    STACK   (Y/N): N                    Y MIN:
    GRID    (Y/N): Y                    Y MAX:
    COLOR   (Y/N): N                    Y DIV:



                                                      F10-Continue
```

Figure 6-7. *Define Chart Menu after data entry*

"CHART TITLE:" entry. Enter **WIDGET MANUFACTURING SALES**, which will be the chart title. For the X axis title, enter **MONTH**; for the Y axis title, enter **$** (see Figure 6-7). Leave other entries as they are (their default values) and press F10. Your chart has now been defined and you should see the Main Menu displayed again.

PRINTING THE CHART

The data to be shown in the chart is now defined. The final step is to print the chart. To get the Printer Menu, enter **5** (Print Chart) and press F10. You can then examine the printer options on the Printer Menu and select the appropriate option values for your chart. As Figure 6-8 shows, the following options are available:

SELECTION NUMBER   Six types of printers are displayed with a corresponding number. Identify your printer and select the corresponding number.

EXPANDED SIZE (Y/N)   The chart can be printed in two sizes. Enter **N** if you wish to print the graph in mal" format. This will be

```
                    PRINTER MENU

        1   IBM GRAPHICS        4   IDS

        2   EPSON               5   NEC

        3   OKIDATA             6   C.ITOH


              SELECTION NUMBER: 3

              EXPANDED SIZE(Y/N): N

              PRINT DATA(Y/N): N

              PRINT TO: LPT1:




                                      F10-Continue
```

Figure 6-8.   *Printer Menu*

about 3×4 inches printed horizontally. If you enter "Y", the graph will be rotated 90 degrees and printed in an expanded format to fill a $8\ 1/2 \times 11$-inch page. The expanded format takes longer to print but is useful if you need a graph that is a full page size. Enter **N** for this printing.

PRINT DATA (Y/N)   In some cases you may wish to have a copy of the data that was used to create the graph. This option can be used to print a copy of the data used for the graph in a columnar format before the graph is printed. The default value is "N". Enter **N** for this printing.

PRINT TO   This is used to select the print device for your system, and is normally "LPT1:" for a parallel printer and "COM1:" for a serial printer. Enter the type for your system. You can also use "CON:" to "print" to the monitor (the output is sent to the monitor instead of the printer).

When you have completed your entries, press F10. The following message will be displayed.

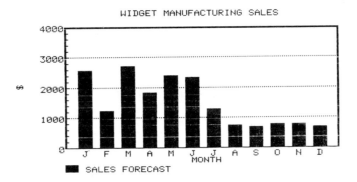

Figure 6-9. *Printout of the first graph*

ABOUT TO PRINT CHART

Press Esc to abandon this operation
Press F10 to continue

This is your last chance to abort the print. (You would press ESC if you wished to abort the printing.) Be sure the printer is on and ready. To initiate the print, press F10. The graph will be printed. You should expect a slow printing, particularly if you selected the expanded size. The printout should look like Figure 6-9.

SAVING THE CHART

Although you have created and printed a graph and chart, it has not been saved, so it can't be printed again or used in another program. To save the chart, select function 4 (Get/Save/Remove) from the Main Menu and press F10. The Get/Save/Remove Menu is shown in Figure 6-10. Notice that there are two Save options on this menu:

SAVE CHART   Saves the data and chart definition and is used if you wish to print or display the chart again at a later time from PFS:GRAPH. The information saved can be read only by PFS:GRAPH.

```
                    GET/SAVE/REMOVE MENU


      1   GET CHART          4   DISPLAY PICTURE

      2   SAVE CHART         5   PRINT PICTURE

      3   SAVE PICTURE       6   REMOVE FILE



               SELECTION NUMBER:

               DIRECTORY OR FILE NAME:




                                             F10-Continue
```

Figure 6-10.   The Get/Save/Remove Menu

SAVE PICTURE   Saves the graphic output in a picture form to use with other programs like **PFS:WRITE**.

Select option 2 (Save Chart) from this Get/Save/Remove Menu. Use TAB to move to the query for the file name. Name this chart "SALES.CHT" (enter **SALES.CHT**). Press F10 and your chart will be saved.

ADDING A SECOND GRAPH

Suppose you have the first six months of sales figures and wish to graph them and compare them with the sales forecast. To do this, you must add a second graph to the chart. From the Main Menu select function 1 (Get/Edit Data) and press F10. From the Get/Edit Data Menu displayed, select option 1 and enter **B** next to "GRAPH (A/B/C/D):". Press F10, and the data entry screen will be displayed for the new graph. Select **M** for the X DATA FORMAT and enter the following sales figures for the graph.

X DATA	Y DATA
1	2251.31
2	1741.19
3	1721.15
4	1485.60
5	1406.97
6	2048.80

Now press F10 to return to the Main Menu, select function **2** (Define Chart), and press F10. When the chart definition is displayed, it will look like it did before, except that now an asterisk will be next to the Graph B entry. Use the TAB key to move to "TYPE" for graph B and enter **BAR**. TAB to "LEGEND" and enter **ACTUAL SALES**. TAB to the "Y AXIS TITLE", and enter **K $** as the correct title. Press F10 to return to the Main Menu.

Finally, select function **3** (Print Chart) from the Main Menu and press F10. Press F10 a second time and the chart will be printed. The printed chart showing both graphs will look like Figure 6-11.

Now try printing this same chart with line graphs instead of bar graphs. From the Main Menu select function **2** (Define Chart) and press F10. To change both type entries from "BAR" to "LINE", TAB to the appropriate field and enter **LINE**. Press F10. Select function **3** (Print

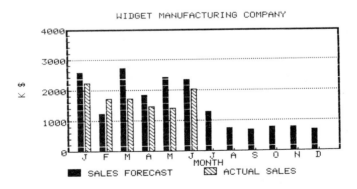

Figure 6-11.   Two graphs on one chart

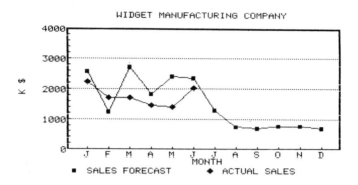

Figure 6-12. *Two line graphs in a chart*

Chart) and press F10 twice to print the chart with line graphs as shown in Figure 6-12. Save this chart under the name **SALES1.CHT** before proceeding to the next section.

CREATING A PIE CHART

From the Main Menu select function **2** (Define Chart) and change the "TYPE" to indicate a pie graph by entering **PIE** for each of the graphs as you did for the line graphs in the previous exercise. Try to print this chart as you did the line graph chart. You will see this error message:

INVALID DATA FOR PIE CHART

If you were to look this up in Appendix A of your PFS:GRAPH manual, you would learn that the previous data does not work for a pie chart because the X DATA identifier value is "M". Only "I"-type identifiers will work for pie charts.

Now create a pie chart that *will* work. From the Main Menu select function **7** (Clear Chart) and press F10 to clear the current chart. Now select function **1** (Get/Edit Data) from the Main Menu and press F10. From the Get/Edit Data Menu select option **1** (Enter/Edit Data) and graph **A**. Press F10. Enter the following data, which represents the sales of six products in a particular year for a company. The X DATA FOR-MAT should be entered as **I**.

X DATA	Y DATA
PRODUCT A	2576
PRODUCT B	1252
PRODUCT C	2742
PRODUCT D	1843
PRODUCT E	2420
PRODUCT F	758

Now press F10, select function **2** (Define Chart), and define a single graph **A**. Enter the "TYPE" as **PIE**, and leave the name at the default "GRAPH A". Press F10. Select function **3** (Print Graph) and press F10. When the Printer Menu is displayed next to the query for "PRINT DATA (Y/N):" enter a **Y**. Then press F10 to print the chart. The chart should look like Figure 6-13.

```
                          GRAPH A

PRODUCT A                 2576
PRODUCT B                 1252
PRODUCT C                 2742
PRODUCT D                 1843
PRODUCT E                 2420
PRODUCT F                 758
```

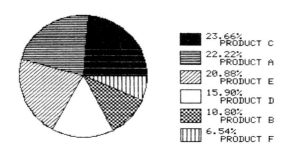

Figure 6-13.   *The pie chart with input data*

STACKED DATA, AREA CHARTS, CUMULATIVE TOTALS, AND GRID LINES

Now suppose Widget sold two products each month and wished to see the relative sales of each product and the total sales each month. This could be done by stacking the values for the sales of each product each month so that the total value displayed showed the total sales for the month. To do this, you will need to clear the data for the pie chart. If you wish to save this chart, you should save it now as you saved your sales chart in an earlier section.

From the Main Menu, select function **7** (Clear Chart) and press F10 to clear the current chart. Select function **1** (Get/Edit Data) and on the next menu select option **1** and graph **A**. Press F10. The Enter/Edit screen is now displayed. Enter **I** for the X DATA FORMAT and enter the following values:

X DATA	Y DATA
1	2576.60
2	1252.30
3	2742.85
4	1843.45
5	2420.37
6	2343.25

Now press F10 to return to the Main Menu. Enter the Graph B data in the same way, except that you select graph **B** on the Get/Edit Data Menu:

X DATA	Y DATA
1	2251.31
2	1741.19
3	1721.15
4	1485.60
5	1406.97
6	2048.80

Now press F10; from the Main Menu select function **2** (Define Chart), and define the chart. Define two graphs. For the first graph, enter **BAR** for the type, a name of **PRODUCT A**, and leave the "CUM" at the default of "N." For the second graph, enter **BAR** again, a legend of **PRODUCT B**, and leave the "CUM" at the default of "N." The "CHART TITLE:" should be **WIDGET MANUFACTURING COMPANY**, the "X-AXIS TITLE:" should be **MONTH**, the "Y-AXIS TITLE:" should be **K $**. Change the "STACK (Y/N):" option to **Y**, and press F10.

Print the chart by selecting function **4** (Print Chart) and pressing F10 twice. The stacked chart should look like Figure 6-14. From this chart you can easily see the total sales for each month as well as the individual sales of each product by month. Now print this same chart without grid lines. Select function **2** (Define Chart) from the Main Menu and press F10. Locate the option "GRID (Y/N):" on this menu and TAB to this option. Change the default "Y" to **N**. Press F10 and then print the chart again as you did in the last paragraph. The chart should look like Figure 6-15. You can also change each graph type to a LINE type by using function **2** (Define Chart) again, entering **LINE**, and leaving all other values the same. The resulting line graph chart is called an *area chart* and shows the totals for each month as the bar graph chart did earlier.

As a final exercise, use the "CUM" option to print a chart showing cumulative totals. Select function **2** (Define Chart) from the Main Menu and locate the "CUM" option for each graph. TAB to this option and change both "CUM" options to **Y**. TAB to the "GRID (Y/N):" option and change this again to the default **N**. Press F10, and print this chart as you did the last two charts in this section. The chart should look like Figure 6-16. Notice that each bar now shows the cumulative year-to-date sales for that product for each month.

OTHER FEATURES

There are many other features in PFS:GRAPH, and you may wish to take some time to explore them now. Charts can be displayed on the monitor, cleared from the computer memory, or recovered from a previously saved chart file.

To display a chart, select function **3** (Display Chart) from the Main Menu and press F10. The current chart that is defined will be displayed. Try this now with the last chart you printed. Charts can be displayed

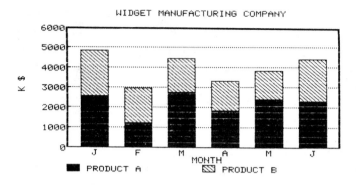

Figure 6-14. *A chart with stacked graphs*

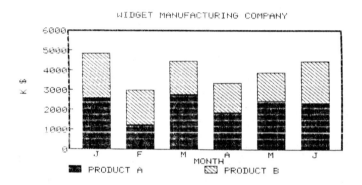

Figure 6-15. *Printing without the grid lines*

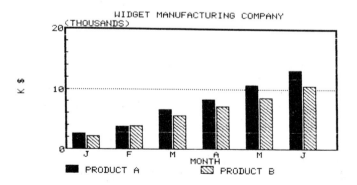

Figure 6-16. *Printing with cumulative totals*

also from the Print Options Menu by selecting the console as the output device (CON:).

There are occasions when you may wish to clear a chart from the computer memory. You have already done this twice in previous exercises to prepare to enter a new chart. This does not erase any chart from the disk (where you saved it as a chart file), but only clears the computer memory so that you can begin to create another chart. Before clearing charts, you should be sure you have saved the current chart in the computer memory. To clear the computer memory of any current chart, select function **7** (Clear Chart) from the Main Menu and press F10.

If you wish to display a chart you previously created and saved (such as the chart of the last section), first clear the current memory (using Clear Chart) and then select function **4** (Get/Edit/Remove) from the Main Menu and press F10. You will then see the Get/Edit/Remove Menu displayed. Select option **1** from this menu, enter the chart name next to "DIRECTORY OR FILE NAME:" and press F10. The chart will now be loaded to the computer memory so it can be printed, plotted, displayed, or edited.

In later chapters you will learn more about PFS:GRAPH: Chapter 11 teaches you how to display data from PFS:FILE with PFS:GRAPH, and in Chapter 12 you will learn how to use data from spreadsheet programs with PFS:GRAPH.

LEAVING PFS:GRAPH

When you have finished printing the graph or graphs you wish to print, select function **8** (Exit PFS:GRAPH) from the Main Menu. This will return you to your computer's operating system, and you will see the operating system prompt:

A>

From this prompt, you can enter the name of any other program you wish to use.

CHAPTER
SEVEN

Using PFS:ACCESS

We live in a world that is exploding with information. John Naisbitt, writing in *Megatrends* (New York: Warner Books, 1982), says that more than 60 percent of us exchange and use information in our work as programmers, teachers, clerks, secretaries, accountants, stockbrokers, managers, insurance people, bureaucrats, lawyers, bankers and technicians. Personal computers enable us to control this information flow. Using a personal computer, a telephone, and some additional hardware and software, anyone can dial into one of the massive databases of information stored on large computers or send an electronic letter to a friend across the country. Electronic communication connects us to external information sources and to other people.

To use the IBM PC for electronic information exchange, only two things are needed: communications software, such as PFS:ACCESS, and a special type of electronic device called a *modem*. The modem enables computer information to be sent and received over telephone lines.

INTRODUCING ELECTRONIC COMMUNICATION

Applications for electronic communication can be divided into two categories. In one category the computer connects people with people; for example, electronic mail, electronic conferencing, and electronic gaming. In the second category the computer connects people with information. These applications include electronic publishing and database searching.

To create and receive electronic mail, you must have an "electronic mailbox" on a computerized system somewhere. One computer system, the host system, stores a collection of these electronic mailboxes. Normally, the host system can be accessed only by using the individual account number and password that are assigned to each user. The account number identifies your mailbox and can be given freely to anyone from whom you wish to receive mail. Your password, in contrast, is confidential and should be given to no one. As illustrated in Figure 7-1, the sender sends the message from a personal computer to the recipient's mailbox on the host system. The message is stored on the host system until the recipient uses his or her computer to access the

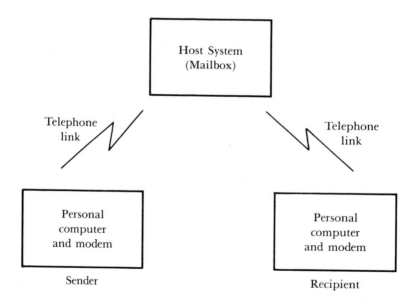

Figure 7-1. Electronic mail system overview

host system and check the mailbox for electronic mail. The host system provides a level of store-and-forward capability for message traffic.

There are basically two types of host systems. One type is the information utility that is accessed from local numbers using special telephone services called *data carrier services*. The second type is the PAMS, or *public access message systems*. A PAMS is a personal computer system that has software facilities for electronic mail and electronic conferencing. In most cities, a dozen or more personal computer owners create these PAMS by leaving their systems connected to telephone lines so other users can "call in" to process electronic mail, hold a conference, or download software. On some systems an electronic mailbox is assigned to a topic rather than to a user, and the mailbox can be used by several individuals interested in that topic. This is the basis of an electronic conferencing system.

Electronic conferencing, another type of people-to-people communication, is rapidly growing in importance because it manages a large collection of information on specific topics across geographic and time zone boundaries. Some of the information utilities provide this conferencing facility. In an electronic conference, a host system manages the conference and personal computers access it. The conferences are organized in topic areas such as medicine, dentistry, computer languages, politics, religion, and gaming. Users can "join" a conference, read the minutes, and quickly become familiar with the discussion. Time zones are not important; messages can be entered into the conference at any time of day. Each time you *log on* to the electronic conference (that is, use your computer to access the conference on the host system), you are automatically given all the new conference messages that have been entered since you last logged on to the conference. On some systems, you can create public or private conferences, "whisper" messages to particular conferees ("whispering" means to send a message that cannot be read by all conference attendees to one or more select attendees) or send conference messages anonymously. Although PFS:ACCESS will not enable you to use your computer as the host system of an electronic conference, you can use PFS:ACCESS to access any conferencing system for which you have the proper account number and access password.

In people-to-information communications, a computer user accesses information stored on other computers. A variety of companies provide extensive banks of information that are sold wholesale in electronic form to services such as DIALOG, Knowledge Index, and BRS. You, in turn, can access these bibliographic services electronically for a fee.

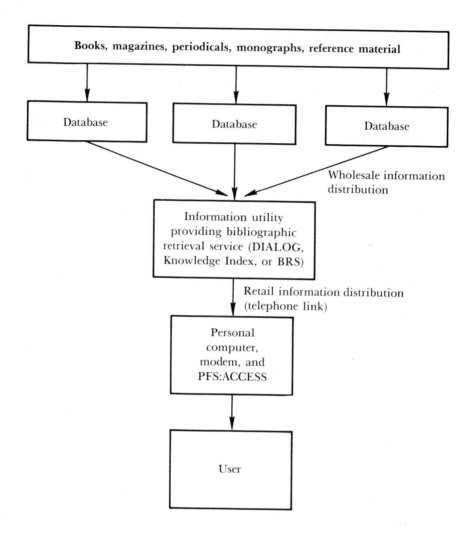

Figure 7-2. Bibliographic retrieval system overview

Applications include patents, searches for foundation grant histories, and titles of books, magazines, and articles on almost any topic (see Figure 7-2).

In another form of people-to-information communication, you can use your computer to order products, perform banking transactions, scan the airline schedules and plan a vacation, or scan the UPI news using keywords that focus on your area of interest.

PAMS

PAMS, or public access message systems, are host systems that can be used for electronic mail and program transfers free of charge. In most cities you can find a dozen or so that are in use. PAMS are frequently called BBS (Bulletin Board Systems) or CBBS (Computerized Bulletin Board Systems). Local user groups and fellow computer users can help you find the telephone numbers of your local PAMS. A good listing of PAMS numbers is included in the book *Electronic Mail and Beyond* by Carl Townsend (Belmont, Calif.: Wadsworth Electronic Publishing Company, 1984). Although numbers for PAMS are frequently busy and you may have trouble getting into one, the systems are free and useful, if only to verify that your modem and communications software work properly.

PAMS are like the broadside publications popular in the early days of America when people created "personal printing presses" in their basements to print their opinions and their visions of America on large sheets of paper. PAMS are used in the new electronic communications culture to distribute and exchange information.

A business can create its own PAMS and use electronic mail and conferencing features to transfer information to salespeople, distributors, or remote offices. If a company sets up its own host system to provide these services, it must use additional hardware and software. Alternatively, corporations can use the host system provided by information utilities. Salespeople and distributors could then use PFS:ACCESS to communicate with the home office through the host system. The remote users would need very little training or computer experience. Since PFS:ACCESS is very easy to use, each salesperson or distributor could have an account number and password on the host system.

THE UTILITIES

Information utilities provide services such as electronic mail, conferencing, electronic purchasing, and database retrieval. Two of the more popular general-purpose information utilities are CompuServe and The Source. The cost of the services depends upon the time of day, the speed (300 or 1200 baud) with which you access the system, and the specific service or database you access. The best rates are available in the evening. Other popular information utilities include Dow Jones News/Retrieval, MCI Mail, and EasyLink.

All of these utilities permit you to use their services with a local telephone line in most cities. The local number connects you to a data carrier service from which you access the utility — all without dialing long-distance. First call the data carrier service with your computer. Once you see the prompt for the data carrier service, you enter the codes necessary to access the information utility you wish to use. You can then enter your account number and password for the utility. Some information utilities now have their own data carrier service, and once you access the data carrier service locally, you are automatically connected to the information utility. In both cases, the cost of the data carrier service is included in the utility cost.

OVERVIEW OF PFS:ACCESS

PFS:ACCESS is a communications program that can connect the IBM PC and compatible machines to information utilities and PAMS. While it is designed to be simple to use, it contains many of the features of its most sophisticated competitors. If you are just starting to use electronic communications, you will find PFS:ACCESS easy to learn and use. If you use electronic communications only occasionally, you will find PFS:ACCESS easy to relearn when you need it. If you are an experienced electronic communications user, you will find PFS:ACCESS to be an easy-to-use alternative for your routine communications.

To use PFS:ACCESS with your computer, you need a modem. Some modems require a special card called an *asynchronous communications adapter*. You will find essential information on setting up modems and other required peripherals in Appendix D. General hardware requirements are specified in Appendix B.

PFS:ACCESS provides the following features:

- There is menu-driven access for eight utilities or services.

- The user can, while connected to a service, scroll forward and backward through the incoming information while the information is being received.

- The incoming information can be stored in a file for analysis later.

- Standard ASCII files from the user's system can be sent to a remote system.

- Documents sent or received can be encrypted, that is, made private using a code to scramble the text.

- Automatic dialing and automatic log-on features are included. This means that you can easily store the telephone number for a utility and all the information necessary to gain access to the utility (such as your account number and password), and this can be retrieved and automatically used by PFS:ACCESS.

- PFS:ACCESS is integrated with PFS:WRITE, PFS:FILE, and PFS:REPORT.

PFS:ACCESS cannot be used to transmit 8-bit binary data files, such as compiled programs, between computers. Only standard ASCII files can be transmitted. ASCII files, or text files, contain only the standard character codes. PFS:ACCESS is not designed to be used as a host system and cannot be operated in an answer mode in which your system can be accessed by other users using PFS:ACCESS.

Like all the other PFS programs, the PFS:ACCESS functions are selected from a single Main Menu (see Figure 7-3). This menu is displayed when you start the program. You will also discover that various keys on the keyboard serve specific functions. These functions are similar to those in other Software Publishing products. Table 7-1 lists the keyboard functions for PFS:ACCESS.

In certain cases, combinations of keys can be used to send commands to the information utility. In these cases, the CTRL key is pressed first

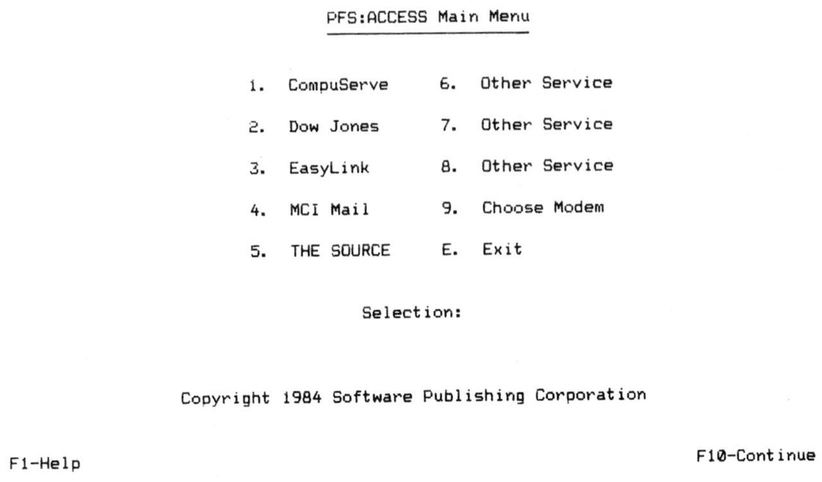

```
                    PFS:ACCESS Main Menu


        1.  CompuServe     6.  Other Service

        2.  Dow Jones      7.  Other Service

        3.  EasyLink       8.  Other Service

        4.  MCI Mail       9.  Choose Modem

        5.  THE SOURCE     E.  Exit


                    Selection:


        Copyright 1984 Software Publishing Corporation


    F1-Help                              F10-Continue
```

Figure 7-3. Main Menu

and held down while the second key is pressed. These codes will vary, depending upon the utility. In general, the following key sequences are valid: CTRL-S, CTRL-Q, CTRL-SCROLL LOCK (see Table 7-1).

Also, when connected to a service, various keys can be used to send commands to PFS:ACCESS. These commands are *not* transmitted to the service and are only used to control or edit information sent to or from the service. These include HOME, PGUP, PGDN, END, INS, DEL, and the CURSOR CONTROL keys (see Table 7-1). You can also use the function keys (F1-F6) to initiate the commands described in Table 7-1.

STARTING PFS:ACCESS

Before beginning, be sure you have already created a backup copy of PFS:ACCESS and configured it for your printer. If you have not done this, refer to Appendix C for the installation instructions. *Be sure to make a backup copy of PFS:ACCESS before starting.*

Just like PFS:WRITE, the operating system will not fit on the disk with the program. With a floppy disk system you will need to boot your system using the system disk and the CTRL, ALT, and DEL keys. After the system is booted, enter the date and then insert the PFS:ACCESS disk in Drive A. If you have a hard disk system, you can install the program on the hard disk (see Appendix C). Start the program by typing

A>**ACCESS** ENTER

Once the program is loaded, you should see the Main Menu shown in Figure 7-3. If you are using a floppy disk system, you can change disks whenever this menu is displayed, but if you are creating or using an automatic log-on sequence, you *must* have the program disk in the default disk drive while you log on to any utility or PAM. With a hard disk system, this is not necessary, since the procedures are stored on the hard disk.

SELECTING THE MODEM

Once the Main Menu is displayed, your first job should be to install PFS:ACCESS for the type of modem you plan to use. (Be sure you have properly installed your modem and communications card as described

Table 7-1. *PFS:ACCESS Keyboard Functions*

Key	Function
F1	Bring up the help menu for PFS:ACCESS
F2	Toggle printer on or off
F3	Disconnect from service
F4	Save automatic log-on
F5	Send a file
F6	Save in a file
F10	Continue the current function
ESC	Cancel an operation and return the user to the Main Menu
TAB	Move the cursor to options on a menu
SHIFT/TAB	Move the cursor backward on a menu
BACKSPACE	Move the cursor one position left and erase the last character typed
CURSOR CONTROL keys	Move the cursor one space in the direction of the arrow; characters are not erased
INS	Toggle between insert and normal mode. In the insert mode, when a character is entered other characters will move to the right to make space for the new character. In normal mode, when a character is entered it will overtype any current character at that location.
PGUP	Move the cursor forward one screen
PGDN	Move the cursor backward one screen
DEL	Delete the character under the cursor location; other characters are moved over to recover the space
HOME	Move the cursor to start of session
END	Return the cursor to the transmission line

Note: The SHIFT key can be used instead of the CONTROL key for any of the operations.

These keys have functions that are interpreted by the remote host system. On most host systems the following key sequences are valid:

CTRL/S	Suspend transmission to or from a utility temporarily (useful if the utility is sending information to you faster than you can read or save it)
CTRL/Q	Resume transmission after a suspension
CTRL/SCROLL LOCK	Interrupt the utility (useful if the utility is sending a long transmission and you decide it is not what you want). This permits you to get immediate control, interrupting whatever is happening.

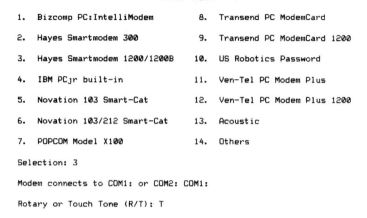

```
                      Choose Modem

   1.   Bizcomp PC:IntelliModem      8.   Transend PC ModemCard

   2.   Hayes Smartmodem 300         9.   Transend PC ModemCard 1200

   3.   Hayes Smartmodem 1200/1200B  10.  US Robotics Password

   4.   IBM PCjr built-in            11.  Ven-Tel PC Modem Plus

   5.   Novation 103 Smart-Cat       12.  Ven-Tel PC Modem Plus 1200

   6.   Novation 103/212 Smart-Cat   13.  Acoustic

   7.   POPCOM Model X100            14.  Others

   Selection: 3

   Modem connects to COM1: or COM2: COM1:

   Rotary or Touch Tone (R/T): T



  F1-Help                  Esc-Main menu              F10-Continue
```

Figure 7-4.   *Selecting the modem*

in Appendix D before you continue.) From the Main Menu, select function **9** (Choose Modem) and press F10. You will then see the Modem Selection Menu shown in Figure 7-4, which lists various modem manufacturers and types. Select the proper code for your modem at the selection prompt. The model number for your modem should be stamped on the modem somewhere — generally at the bottom or on the rear panel of the modem. If you have a built-in modem, check the manufacturer's manual. You must also select which computer port the modem will use (COM1: or COM2:). In most systems, you should leave this at the default, COM1:. If you are using a serial printer for COM1: or another device for this port, select COM2:. On the query for Rotary or Touch Tone, use "T" if you have a touch tone phone and "R" if you have a rotary dial phone. Use the TAB key to move the cursor to the proper option and enter the alternative value. Once all the values are entered, press F10 to save the values. Your modem type is saved as a part of your program. It is not necessary to reenter your modem type each time you start the program. If you need help at any time, press F1. You can now begin to access an information utility or PAMS.

FIRST SESSION

To begin using a service, you will need the following:

- Telephone number of the service.

- Your account number for the service.

- A password for the service.

- To access The Source, you will also need the two-digit number for the computer system to which your account is assigned.

The Source will be the example since it is one of the most popular information utilities. An access package for The Source can be purchased at many computer stores and book dealers. If your PFS:ACCESS contains a subscription form for The Source, you can also purchase an access package by filling out this form and mailing it in. This purchased access package will contain a password, account number, and the two-digit number for the computer system you should use, such as "47". This number can be found by checking The Source manual for your log-on procedure. It will contain the area code for The Source's computer (301) and a number such as @C 30147 for system "47". For this demonstration, you will need an account number and password. You can also check your PFS:ACCESS manual to see i f a free demonstration account number and password are listed for The Source utility. If so, you can use these for the demonstration.

In most cities, The Source can be accessed using a local telephone number. This number will be for some type of data carrier service (such as Telenet), which will connect you to The Source. To find your local Telenet number, call the Telenet Customer Support at 1-800-336-0437. Use the local telephone number for your city for this demonstration. Note the data carrier service number, as you will need it during the demonstration.

For your demonstration, you should define a specific goal so that you can keep your on-line costs low. Your first goal could be simply to log on to the system and then log off again. To begin your first session, select function **5** (The Source) from the PFS:ACCESS Main Menu and wait for the service information screen to be displayed (Figure 7-5). The cursor will be on the second line, which is a query for the telephone number. Type in the Telenet access number. Use dashes or spaces if you wish. If you must dial 9 before dialing an outside number, type **9** before

```
                        Service Information

        Service name: THE SOURCE

        Telephone number: 295-3028

        Create automatic sign-on (Y/N): Y



                      Communications Settings

        Modem speed (300 or 1200): 1200
        Data bits (7 or 8): 7
        Stop bits (1 or 2): 1
        Parity (none, odd, even, mark, space): EVEN
        Half or full duplex (H/F): F


            Automatic sign-on - Press F10 to continue

    F1-Help                     Esc-Main menu              F10-Continue
```

Figure 7-5. Service information screen

the access number. This will instruct PFS:ACCESS to dial 9, wait two seconds, and then dial the access number. TAB the cursor to the third line and enter **Y** for the creation of an automatic log-on. Once you have created an automatic log-on for a service, you won't need to enter the telephone number, account number, and password each time you wish to access the service. PFS:ACCESS "remembers" this information and automatically enters it each time you use the service.

TAB the cursor to the next line, and if the modem speed is not correct for your modem, enter the correct modem speed. Leave the remainder of the settings at their default values: Data bits=7, Stop bits=1, Parity= Even and Half or full duplex=F. Press F10. After a few seconds, the PFS:ACCESS program will begin dialing the number. Once the connection is made, the screen will change and some indication will be given that you are now connected to the data carrier service (see Figure 7-6). (If you used the data carrier service for Telenet instead of the Source's data carrier service, you will not see "SOURCENET"—only an indication that the connection is completed.) Notice that two solid lines divide the screen into sections. Below the line at the bottom of the screen is the status line where messages from PFS:ACCESS and help messages are displayed. Above the status line is the *on-line area* that displays the dialogue with the remote system. The cursor will appear in the on-line area.

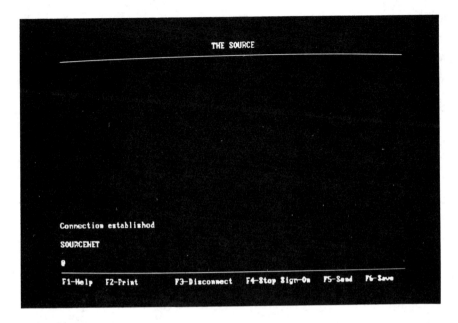

THE SOURCE

Connection established

SOURCENET

@

F1-Help   F2-Print   F3-Disconnect   F4-Stop Sign-On   F5-Send   F6-Save

Figure 7-6. *The terminal screen*

Press ENTER twice. This enables the computer at the other end of the line (the computer used by the data carrier service) to determine some basic technical information—such as the modem speed—about your system. If you are using Telenet, you will see the TERMINAL prompt from the data carrier service (SOURCENET does not ask for your terminal type):

Connection Established

TELENET
503 115C

TERMINAL=

If the TERMINAL query is displayed, press ENTER again. You should then see the "@" prompt (this prompt is displayed for either data carrier service). This is a request for the area code and computer within that area code that Telenet is to access. Type in the following:

@C 301XX ENTER

"XX" is the computer number for the specific system assigned to your account and password. This should be in the documentation you received with your account and password. If you are using a demonstration account, the value for "XX" is normally 47.

You will enter this information regardless of where you are dialing *from*. This is the code for the main computer of The Source. (The data carrier service system in Virginia can access many computers besides The Source.) It tells Telenet to access system "47" in area code "301", the computer for The Source. Almost immediately, you will see The Source prompt (>) verifying the connection and requesting your account number and password. Type in the following:

>**ID YYYYYY *ZZZZZZ*** ENTER

where "YYYYYY" is your account number (such as "TCE016") and "*ZZZZZZ*" is your password (such as "ROGER").

You should now be connected to The Source. A Source menu should be displayed, as shown in Figure 7-7. Press F4 to save the log-on sequence you just entered.

The Source should then respond with a few news items about the latest changes and display a menu. This menu includes an option to go to the command level. Select this option (option **6** in Figure 7-7). You will then see the ">" prompt. Enter **off** and press ENTER. The Source will then sign you off, telling you the amount of time you used on the system.

You have now signed off The Source, but are still connected to the data carrier service. Once you have signed off The Source, press F3 (Disconnect). You will then see a warning message that you are disconnecting. Press F10 and the computer will "hang up" the phone and PFS:ACCESS will return you to the Main Menu.

The PFS:ACCESS manual discusses the information utilities listed on the Main Menu. You can study this manual and the variety of available books and articles on information services (including *Answers Online* by B. Newlin, Osborne/McGraw-Hill, 1985) to find the service or services that best meet your needs. Once you have made this decision, you should fill out the necessary forms and apply to the utility.

If you must mail in an application to a utility to get an account, you might wish to access some local PAMS to gain some experience using PFS:ACCESS while waiting to receive your information utility account. To access a PAMS, you must know its telephone number and modem

```
TELENET
503 115A

TERMINAL=

@c 301 24


301 24 CONNECTED
Connected to THE SOURCE
)
TELENET
503 115A

TERMINAL=

@c 30124


301 24 CONNECTED
Connected to THE SOURCE
) id tce016 rocky
TCE016 (user 21) logged in Thursday, 16 Aug 84 01:39:12.
Welcome, you are connected to THE SOURCE.
Last login Wednesday, 15 Aug 84 01:09:12.

(C) COPYRIGHT SOURCE TELECOMPUTING CORPORATION 1984.

AIRSCHED, BIZDATE, SPORTS, BULLETIN, SFILES,
TRAVEL, TODAY, BARTER, SEVERAL GAMES AND WIRE
SERVICES WILL NOT BE AVAILABLE FROM 4 TO 6 P'
(EDT) ON 08/16/84 DUE TO MAINTENANCE.


-)


WELCOME TO THE SOURCE

1   USING THE SOURCE
2   TODAY
3   BUSINESS UPDATE
4   THE SOURCE MAIN MENU
5   WHAT'S NEW
6   COMMAND LEVEL

Enter item number or HELP 6

-) off
TCE016 (user 21) logged out Thursday, 16 Aug 84 01:40:08.
Time used: 00h 01m connect.

Wait...
Bye


301 24 DISCONNECTED 00 00

@
```

Figure 7-7. *Demonstration of The Source*

speed. Often you can get this information from local computer dealers or user group members. Now, load PFS:ACCESS and select function **6** (Other Services) from the Main Menu. When the Service Information Menu is displayed, enter the information for the PAM system. Press F10 to start the dialing. Once the PAM system answers the phone, you may have to enter more information, depending upon the PAMS. You can save the log-on sequence for a PAMS, just as you saved The Source sequence, by pressing the F4 key.

ADDING AND EDITING SERVICES

Once the log-on sequence of PAMS or an information utility has been added, PFS:ACCESS can automatically access the service—you don't have to enter the telephone number, account number, and password each time you dial. This will only work for modems with auto-dial. If you use a modem without auto-dial or an acoustic-coupled modem, you will still have to dial the number manually each time you access a service or PAMS.

Suppose you originally used a demonstration account on The Source and now have a valid Source account and password. You wish to add the correct log-on sequence with your account information to your program. From the Main Menu, select function **5** (The Source) again and press F10. You will see the Service Information Menu. The cursor will be at the Service name, but you can alter this if you wish. To change the telephone number, press TAB once and then type in the new phone number. TAB the cursor to the request to create an automatic sign-on and enter a **Y**. Press TAB again to move the cursor to the modem speed request and enter the correct modem speed. Now press F10. The system will begin to dial the number. When the prompt for the data carrier service is displayed, press ENTER and wait for the prompt again:

Connection Established

TELENET
503   115C

TERMINAL= ENTER
@

Enter the correct area code and the computer system within the area code (use the information that came with your Source user's manual, *not* the numbers listed here):

@C **30147** ENTER

Earlier, you may have used a demonstration account with a computer system number of "47". This may not be The Source computer number now assigned to your account. Check the information that came with your account number and password to see which computer system number you have been assigned to use. While you can send mail to or receive mail from any Source user regardless of the computer system he or she is using, you must always dial into the particular Source computer system that has your account and password information.

Once The Source connection is established, enter your account number and password. When The Source main menu is displayed, indicate the log-on is complete and press F4 to save the information you have entered as a part of the automatic log-on. If you have a Source account, try sending a message to yourself on The Source using the directions in The Source user's manual. After you "send" a message, it takes a few minutes before the message is in your mailbox. Information about using The Source or other information utilities is beyond the scope of this book, but you will find many helpful books and magazine articles on using all of the information utilities.

SENDING FILES

This section describes how files are sent. If you have a valid account number and password to The Source, you can perform this example; otherwise, you can only read it to understand the process.

To save time and money, write and edit your mail off-line, and then transmit your completed letters to The Source. You can do this by creating your letter first and writing the letter to a disk file. This can be done with any word processor, including PFS:WRITE. Once the letter is ready (such as the TEST.LTR you created in Chapter 2), load PFS:ACCESS and log on to the utility as before. Examine the main Source menu and select the command that will return you to the command mode. You should then see The Source prompt:

>

Prepare to send your letter by accessing the electronic mail feature. This is done by entering

>**MAIL S** ENTER

The service will then request the account number of the recipient. Enter your own account number for the recipient (send the letter to yourself) and when you see a prompt "SUBJECT", this is a request for a short, one-line description of the contents of your letter. Enter **TEST**. Once The Source requests the text, press F5. You will then see this prompt from PFS:ACCESS:

Name of text file to send:
Privacy Code:

Enter the name of your letter file with any appropriate disk designator such as:

Name of text file to send: **B:TEST.LTR**

Press F10. You will then see your message scroll on the screen as it is transmitted to The Source. After the message is transmitted, you need to enter the code that tells the utility that the message is completed. For The Source, enter **.S**. This can either be stored as the final character on a line by itself or entered manually after the message transmission is completed. For now, enter it manually:

.S ENTER

You can also enter a privacy code to encrypt the message. To read the message the recipient would need to have **PFS:ACCESS** and the code.

Saving Information to a File

You may frequently wish to save the dialogue of a session to a disk file so you can read it later. Many users save all sessions to a disk file as a backup precaution. To save information to a file, place a blank disk in the disk drive and press F6. You will then see the following prompts on the status line:

Save text in file:
Privacy Code:

Enter the file name with the appropriate disk drive designator. Since no privacy code is needed, press ENTER and the dialogue will be saved to disk in the named disk file. Press F6 to stop saving the dialogue. You can save multiple files during a single utility session, giving each a different name.

Using Privacy Codes

Privacy codes can be used to encrypt a message sent to another computer so that only a PFS:ACCESS user who knows the code can read the message. Repeat the exercise of sending a message to yourself, but this time use a privacy code. When The Source gives you the prompt for "TEXT", press F5 again. This time enter the name of your letter file **B:TEST.LTR** and a privacy code of **SUNSHINE**. The letter will be transmitted to The Source as before, but you will notice that the text is garbled and meaningless as it is displayed on the screen. Enter **.S** to end the letter, and wait until it appears in your mailbox on the utility.

When you come back to your mailbox and find your letter, it will still be garbled. To read it, save it to a file as SOURCE.DOC using F6 and use the same privacy code, **SUNSHINE**, that you used before. Then you should log off The Source, return to the Main Menu of PFS:ACCESS, and exit PFS:ACCESS using function **E** (Exit). Once you have returned to the operating system, enter the DOS **TYPE** command to read the received file, SOURCE.DOC. It will no longer be garbled and should look like the original letter.

USING INFORMATION UTILITIES EFFICIENTLY

Remember that you will be billed for the time you are connected to an information utility. Consider these strategies for saving both time and money.

Plan your on-line sessions ahead of time and develop specific strategies for your utility use. For example, when many users discover a new feature on a utility, they cannot resist the temptation to immediately try it out. If you have just found yourself in a CompuServe SIG group, for example, you may get excited and try various command options to "see what happens." Resist the temptation. Instead, log off and read the instructions (for example, the CompuServe SIG manual) and *then* try the feature. Define your short- and long-term goals in using utilities; you may find that some of these objectives can be better met by using other methods. In addition to planning sessions ahead of time, you should keep a logbook of your time on the utility and how it is used. Most utilities will *not* give you a cost breakdown of each of your sessions at the end of the month; nor can you get this breakdown on-line. If you want records, you will need to keep them yourself. This is why many users keep a logbook. A logbook can verify billing, track interesting projects, and verify if your use of the utility is cost-effective.

In addition, always keep a record of the total session dialogue on a disk file or printout for a few days. If an error is made, you can often recover your costs. For example, if the order feature of a bibliographic retrieval service is not working and you try to order a document, you may be able to recover the session cost if no message was given at log-on that the order service was not working. If you had saved a copy of the dialogue to a disk or printer, you could send the utility a record of what you did to verify your claim.

Organize your disks and file names. This helps when you are on-line and cannot remember the file name you wish to transmit or the file names you have already used to save text. To reduce electronic mail costs, you should create and edit your documents off-line and send them as files.

Here are a few more hints on using PFS:ACCESS:

- To remove a service, use the Main Menu and enter the function for the desired service. When the Service Information Menu is displayed, enter blanks for the service name and press F10. PFS:ACCESS will display a warning message before deleting the service and give you a chance to escape.

- You can enter telephone numbers with as many digits as will fit on the display. To indicate a pause in the number, enter a comma. Each comma equals about a two-second wait, and you can use more than one comma. This is useful if you need to dial "9" to get an outside line. You can also use parentheses, hyphens, or spaces to clarify the number however you wish. For example,

9,1-(415)555-5555

- If you select the acoustic modem from the Main Menu, you will need to dial the number manually after pressing F10 from the Service Information Menu. Once connected to the desired number, you will need to press F10 again.

- The dialogue with the host system can be printed at any time by using the F2 key to toggle the printer on or off. It is always a good idea to print your information or to save the information to a disk file.

- You can always abort an automatic log-on by pressing the F4 key at any time during the log-on.

- You can change an automatic log-on by entering a **Y** next to the item "Create Automatic Sign-on (Y/N):" on the Service Information Menu. After the new log-on procedure has been completed, the old automatic log-on sequence is automatically overwritten by the new procedure.

- To send or receive mail, your recipient must have a valid account on the service and you must know the account number. Exceptions to this include only MCI Mail and the Mailgram service. You can give anyone your account number, but should keep your password secret and change it often. You may wish to print your account number on your business cards and stationery.

LEAVING PFS:ACCESS

To leave a utility, *always* sign off using the appropriate log-off command such as OFF, LOGOFF, or BYE. If you fail to do this and simply disconnect using the F3 key, you will still be billed for the few minutes it takes before the utility has recognized you have signed off. With most utilities, this is about five to fifteen minutes. Most utilities operate in this way in case a person is dropped off-line accidentally. If you are dropped off-line accidentally (for example by pressing F3 by mistake during a session) it is possible to log back on to the service within this short time without losing information you might have been using.

When you have finished your electronic communications, select function **E** (Exit) from the Main Menu. This will return you to your computer's operating system, and you will see the operating system prompt

A>

From this prompt, you can enter the name of any other program you wish to use.

PART
TWO

Working With PFS:FILE
Databases

CHAPTER
EIGHT

Designing Files
With PFS:FILE

At this point you have already used PFS:FILE to design a few files. You are probably eager to start using it for productive work. To do so you must first answer several questions for yourself:

- What type of records do you wish to store?
- What type of information (items) about these records do you need to store?
- How do you design your files to support what you need to do?

This chapter explores and answers these questions.

PLANNING YOUR OBJECTIVES

Your first objective should be to decide what information you actually need in order to make your decisions. Having too much information is almost as bad as having too little, because you could have difficulty finding the data you need for making decisions. You will find yourself drowning in a sea of information. PFS:FILE makes it easy to redesign files to include extra information you may need to add (or delete). So when you first design a file, avoid putting more information in it than you need. You can always add more information later, if you find it necessary.

If you are currently creating reports, use them as a starting point to assess how efficiently you are designing them. Ask yourself two questions: What information do you need that is missing from these reports? What information is included in these reports that you do not need? Notice that this analysis reverses your actual operating procedure. When you are *using* the files you design, you start with information, and the final output does not come into existence until sometime later. In this analysis, by contrast, you start by analyzing your output — identifying goals and determining what kind of reports will serve your needs — and work backward to determine the type of information you will enter in your files.

Before designing your files, you should design your reports. Determine beforehand how they should look in their printed form. You might even want to type some dummy reports that show how you expect your final reports to appear. The design of your form should make it easy for anyone entering the information to visualize what is happening, so you should examine the forms you are using for input before you start using the computer. You may wish to copy these to make it easier for users to adapt to the computer system. For example, if you have an inquiry system in which you keep track of prospective customers and each prospect is listed on a 3 × 5 card, you might wish to design your form exactly like the prospect card you are currently using, or at least use the card as a starting point in your form design.

Remember, as a user you can visualize information stored by PFS:FILE as one or more items in a file of collected records. You use the PFS:FILE *form* that appears on the screen to enter, retrieve, or display information for each record. When you design the form, you determine what information — that is, which items — will be saved for each record.

DESIGNING FILES

When you are beginning to design your files, there are several factors to consider:

1. What items do you need to store for each record?
2. What is the size of each of these items?

3. In what order will the items be entered?

4. In what order will the items be printed on labels or reports?

5. What items will you use to control the sort and retrieval of information?

6. What type of retrieval do you intend to use? (Will you need lengthy retrieval specifications for a particular item?)

Let's look more closely at these six factors, using examples to illustrate each one's importance.

First, you should define only the items you will need for your file and avoid using extra items. When, for example, in Chapter 5, you designed a file to hold modem products, it might have been tempting to put the manufacturers' addresses with each record (see Figure 8-1) so that you could use the addresses to create a mailing to the manufacturers. However, such a use is not really compatible with the characteristics of the program. A manufacturer's address would have to be entered for each product, even if that same address had already been entered for another one of its products. If we were then to do a mailing, the manufacturers

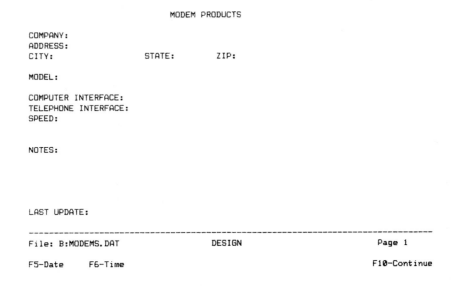

Figure 8-1. *Modem file with "ADDRESS:" added*

for which more than one product is listed would receive multiple mailings. For this reason, the address was left out of the file created in Chapter 5. (If you know you will need to mail something to each of the manufacturers, you should put the addresses in a separate file that contains only the addresses of modem manufacturers. So when designing your file, first consider how the file will be used and enter only the items that support this use.)

Second, when designing your file, you must take into consideration the size of the items you will need. You should design your file so that for each item you have enough space for the largest value that you expect to assign to that item. PFS:FILE is very good in this respect. Leaving a large space for an address or adding a second address line does not necessarily make a file larger. The form can be designed with items anywhere on the page; item values can be of any size as long as they fit on the page, and the items can be moved later without loss of the item values that have already been entered. This storage technique, called *free-form,* is a great asset in designing files.

It should be noted, however, that file storage for each record is allocated in 128-byte blocks. Each page of the form will use one or more 128-byte blocks. Pages containing many items or long character string values for items can take several blocks of storage. If you add extra pages to your form, you will find you can store fewer records on a disk. Try to store everything on one page if you can.

Third, the order of the items on the page should be as close as possible to the order in which the information will be printed. For example, in Chapter 4 the **PROSPECTS.DAT** file design contained the last name first. This sequence enabled efficient retrieval by last name (as described under the fifth factor, later). However, this sequence made it impossible to print mailing labels in a first name/last name sequence, such as:

MARY CHRISTMAS

If you had wished to print the labels in a more conventional manner, you could have designed the form with the first name first (as in Figure 8-2), and then, before printing, you could have inserted an "S" on the report specification next to "LASTNAME:". This would have sorted the addresses for the mailing labels by the last name and printed the first line of each address with the first name first.

Fourth, the order of the items on the page should be as close as possible to the order in which information will be entered by later users of the form. For example, suppose you have run an advertisement in a

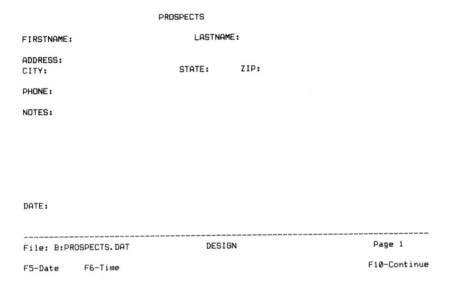

```
                          PROSPECTS

         FIRSTNAME:                    LASTNAME:

         ADDRESS:
         CITY:                STATE:      ZIP:

         PHONE:

         NOTES:




         DATE:

         ------------------------------------------------------------------------
         File: B:PROSPECTS.DAT           DESIGN                     Page 1

         F5-Date      F6-Time                                   F10-Continue
```

Figure 8-2. *Prospect file with FIRSTNAME first*

magazine for several new products your company has developed. As you receive the responses, they are entered into a file such as the one shown in Figure 8-3. If the information must be entered in the sequence of address first and product second, there will be a lot of wasted cursor motion as the user enters the address and then moves the cursor back to the "PRODUCT:" item. When planning the order of your items, imagine the user actually using the input information and how it will be entered. Plan your item order to minimize wasted time and effort.

Fifth, before designing your file you should decide what item you will generally be using to retrieve the record. You should then place this item in the upper left of the form; that is, you make it the first item in the form. PFS uses any item in the upper left of the form as a *key* to access records in the file. When you use the key item for retrieval, PFS:FILE can go directly to it. If you use other items for retrieval, PFS:FILE will take longer because it will have to scan the entire file and extract those that match your criteria. In Chapter 2 LASTNAME was used as the key in order to quickly retrieve individual addresses. Although the file design of Figure 8-2 is excellent for printing mailing labels, quick retrievals can only be made on the first name.

Finally, in designing your form, you should also leave sufficient space

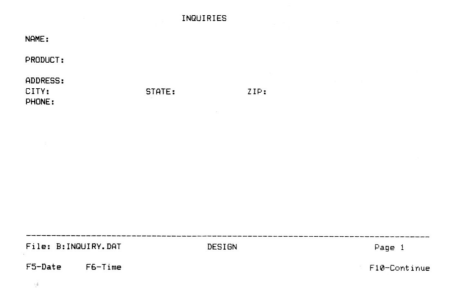

```
                              INQUIRIES

     NAME:

     PRODUCT:

     ADDRESS:
     CITY:                  STATE:           ZIP:
     PHONE:




     ------------------------------------------------------------------
     File: B:INQUIRY.DAT            DESIGN                    Page 1

     F5-Date     F6-Time                              F10-Continue
```

Figure 8-3. Inquiry file with address broken

for any type of retrieval specification you anticipate. Remember that the same form that you use to enter information is also used for retrieval, so the space beside each item must hold sufficient information for any planned retrieval. For example, since ZIP codes for locations in the U.S.A. are only five digits, you would normally leave space for only five characters. However, if you wanted to retrieve information using

ZIP: =10000..90000

which would select all records with ZIP codes between 10000 and 90000 inclusive, you would need to design your form with thirteen spaces for the ZIP. In Figure 8-4, a form is shown that has only five spaces for the ZIP code, making it impossible to retrieve or print on a ZIP range.

Chapter 9 looks at how to do complex searches and how the retrieval works. You should read that chapter before going too far with your form design. Some of the factors involved in the file design involve compromises; for example, we have seen that some level of compromise is necessary in deciding whether to put the last or first name first when designing the file. All of the factors must be considered, and you will need to decide which are most important.

```
                          INQUIRIES

     NAME:

     PRODUCT:

     ADDRESS:
     CITY:                    STATE:  ZIP:    PHONE:
```

```
------------------------------------------------------------------------
   File: B:INQUIRY.DAT            DESIGN                   Page 1

   F5-Date      F6-Time                              F10-Continue
```

Figure 8-4.   *Inquiry file with too little room for ZIP*

DESIGNING MULTI-PAGE FORMS

Each record is stored as one or more pages of a form. You can store as many as 100 items on a page and can use a total of 32 pages for a record. An example might be a medical form for a patient. The pages could represent different types of information. One page could be insurance information; another page, patient history; and another (perhaps the first page), general information. Using this method you could store up to 3200 items of information for each patient. You will not be able to store forms for many patients on a single disk, but this might be adequate for a small clinic. If you are using a hard disk, the space limitations are not as critical, and the idea of using multiple pages on a form for this type of application might be even more attractive. Of course, you should not store more information than you actually intend to use.

In designing a multi-page form, you can use the page control keys to move between pages:

PGDN   Moves to the next page of the form

PGUP   Moves to the previous page of the form

As you design a multi-page form, you can move between pages at any time to change or alter the form design. As you move from page to page, you will see the active page number displayed at the bottom of the screen. If an asterisk is displayed with the number, it means there are additional form pages after the current page.

As a rule, keep your pages functionally designed. A user should be able to know that certain types of information are on certain pages. This will spare the reader the need to browse through several pages to determine where specific information might be stored.

You can use a notebook to keep track of forms and data files. Use a three-ring binder, keeping a printed copy of each form in the notebook with some type of index so you can locate any forms of interest quickly. Also use this same notebook to keep track of the data files you are using and the name of each.

CHAPTER
NINE

Merging and Extracting Records With PFS:FILE

This chapter looks at some advanced procedures that use PFS:FILE: selecting records based on criteria from a file and performing extractions and merges. *Merging* is the process of adding records from one or more files to a single file. *Extraction*, the reverse process, involves taking records that meet a certain criterion from one file and moving them to another file. During extraction the records in the original file may be removed from the original file. You will start with an exercise in merging and add new records to the file B:PROSPECT.DAT.

MERGING

Merges are used to combine records in two or more files to a single file. To do a merge, you will need at least two disk drives or a hard disk drive. In most cases, you will not need a new diskette. Just be sure you have enough room on your data disk for both the new file and some expansion room for the "master" file—the existing file into which the new file will be merged. Of course, if you are using a hard disk, the new file and the master file will both be on the hard disk. You should always create a copy of your master file before starting.

One practical use for a merge might be to add small working files to a master file. The small working files will be easier and faster to sort, print, and update. Once the working files are correct, they can be merged with the master file. For example, suppose you have a master mailing list and you wish to add another fifty names. The best approach would be to create an empty file with a design just like that of your master file. You would then load your new records to this file, after which you would be able to print the file, and then edit and print it again until it is correct. Once the new file is correct, you would merge it to the master file.

To start the merge, bring up the PFS:FILE Main Menu and select function 3 (Copy). Use B:PROSPECT.DAT as the master file and copy its form design to a new file, B:TEMP.DAT (this will be a temporary working file). Enter the name of your master file and any necessary disk designator (here, **B:PROSPECT.DAT**). Press F10. You will then see the Copy Function Menu (see Figure 9-1). Select function 1 (Copy Design Only) and enter the name of your *new* file and any necessary disk designator on the Copy Function Menu as **B:TEMP.DAT**. Press F10 and the form will be copied to the new file. B:TEMP.DAT will not contain any records.

Now on the Main Menu *change* the file name currently displayed to

```
                    COPY FUNCTION MENU



            1   COPY DESIGN ONLY

            2   COPY SELECTED FORMS

            3   COPY WHOLE FILE



            SELECTION NUMBER: 1

            NEW FILE NAME: B:TEMP.DAT




                                         F10-Continue
```

Figure 9-1. The Copy Menu

```
                    PROSPECTS

    LASTNAME: JONES              FIRSTNAME: TOM

    ADDRESS: 509 FIRST STREET
    CITY: MADISON           STATE: WI   ZIP: 53714

    PHONE:

    NOTES: AGRICULTURAL ENGINEER




    DATE:

    ---------------------------------------------------------------------------
    File: B:TEMP.DAT               FORM 1                    Page 1

    F2-Print Form     F5-Date     F6-Time                    F10-Continue
```

Figure 9-2.   The first address for merging

the name of your new file (B:TEMP.DAT), select the Add function (**2**), and press F10 to begin adding records to your new file. Add the two records shown in Figures 9-2 and 9-3. Edit and print this file as necessary until it is correct. The advantage of using this small, temporary file is that you can work with it to make corrections more easily than when using the larger file. Sorts and retrievals will take less time, and your listings will contain only the new addresses, which are the only ones that would contain errors. Any corrections or changes that must be made to old addresses should be made directly on the master file either before starting the merge or after the merge is completed.

Once the new B:TEMP.DAT file is correct, from the Main Menu select the Copy function (**3**) again and keep the name of the new file (B:TEMP.DAT) on the Main Menu. On the Copy Function Menu, select option **2** (Copy Selected Forms), and enter the name of your master file, **B:PROSPECT.DAT**, next to "NEW FILE NAME:". Press F10 and you will see the retrieval specification screen. Since you wish *all* records copied from the new file *to* the master, leave this screen blank and press F10 again. Each of the new records will be copied to the master file, and as each record is copied, it will be displayed on the screen. When the Copy function is completed, press F10 again. From the Main Menu select function 4 (Search/Update) and enter the file name **B:PROSPECT.DAT.**

```
                      PROSPECTS
      -------------------------------------------------
      LASTNAME: WIGGENBOTTOM         FIRSTNAME: BARRY

      ADDRESS: 1845 THIRD STREET
      CITY: RALEIGN |-|              STATE: NC   ZIP: 27605

      PHONE:

      NOTES: MANUFACTURING PLANT MANAGER




      DATE:

      -----------------------------------------------------------------
      File: B:TEMP.DAT              FORM 2                    Page 1

      F2-Print Form    F5-Date    F6-Time              F10-Continue
```

Figure 9-3. *The second address for merging*

Press F10 and examine your new file. Notice that the data that was already in the destination file has not been destroyed by the copying of records to the file.

In summary, the following steps are used to merge files. Only the last step is the actual merge operation:

1. Using the Copy Design Only function of the Copy Function Menu, create a new file from the old file.

2. Add your new records to this new file.

3. After this new file has been edited and proofread, use the Copy Selected Forms option from the Copy Function Menu to merge it with the old file.

CREATING SELECTION CRITERIA

After you have created a file, it may contain several hundred records. Scanning an entire file to find a particular record wastes time, so it is better to choose information about the records you are trying to find and use that information to find additional information about the record.

For example, somewhere in your file of mailing addresses is an address for Tom Jones. You know the first and last names, and using this information, you wish to locate the entire address from the file. Here the key (the item to locate the complete record) would be the last name.

PFS:FILE can use any item in the file as a key to locate the desired records quickly. PFS:FILE uses this item to build an index that is used to locate records. However, in order to use an item as a key, you must place it in the upper-left corner of the form. *Whatever item name you place in the upper left of your form is used by PFS:FILE for the key.* If you are trying to locate a record using this item, PFS:FILE will search the index and find it quickly. PFS:FILE indexes only key item names. If you use any other item on the form to find the record (or records), then PFS:FILE will *not* have it in an index; it will have to search through every form in the entire file until it finds a record matching the specified criteria — a very slow process. On the average, it will need to search through half of the file to find the record matching the criteria. The solution is simple. Whatever item you intend to use most often to retrieve records you make the key item by placing it in the upper-left corner of the file, so that it will be used by PFS:FILE to build the index.

PFS:FILE and PFS:REPORT use the same procedure for doing any type of retrieval. The procedure is the same whether records are being selected to print, to edit, to be removed from the file, or to be included in a tabular report (PFS:REPORT). Once you have learned how to do retrievals, you will find it easy to display, edit, remove, or print any desired record or group of records in your file.

Retrievals are done by means of a blank *retrieval form*, which is filled in with information that is then matched by the program to find the records to be retrieved. The information entered into this retrieval form is called the *retrieval specification*. There are five types of retrieval specifications. Each can be used separately, or they can be used on a single form in combination. The five types are

1. Full item match: The record is retrieved only if the value of the item in the record *exactly* matches the item value on the retrieval form.

2. Partial item match: The record is retrieved if the item value in the record matches your criterion or criteria to the specified degree. For example, you may not know exactly how a name is spelled, but

you know the first or last letters of a name. Using these letters and the partial item match techniques, you could still locate the record.

3. Numeric item match: The record is retrieved if the numeric value of the item either matches, exceeds, or is less than (according to which special symbol you use) the numeric value of the retrieval specification. This method is *not* the same as a full item match, for the rules for determining if a numeric match exists are different from the rules used to determine a full item match. This will be clarified with examples later in the chapter.

4. Numeric range match: The record is retrieved if the numeric value of the item is within a range given by the retrieval specification.

5. The NOT match: The record is retrieved if the value of the item does *not* match the retrieval specification value.

To help you understand each of these, here are some examples.

PFS:FILE always stores information in a file as one or more characters. This is true whether the information consists of numbers or letters. For retrieval purposes, these item values are considered either character strings or numbers. A name, for example, would be a *character string*. (A character string is defined as one or more alphanumeric characters; for example, "JOHN SMITH" is a character string.) An inventory part number, if used in a PFS:FILE, would be stored as a character string but could be retrieved by treating the inventory part number as a character string *or* a number. Full item retrievals and partial item retrievals treat the item value as a character string. Numeric item retrievals and numeric range retrievals treat the item value as a number. The NOT retrieval specification can be used with either numeric or character string retrievals.

Full Item Matches

In a full item match, the retrieval specification is used to enter a string of characters that must exactly match the value of an item in order for the record to be retrieved. If the match is exact, the record is retrieved. The full item match can retrieve either a single, unique record or all records sharing a specified item value. That is, you could use this method to find a single specific record in the file (such as the address of Tom Jones), or you could enter, say, ZIP code "97212" in order to retrieve all records with a ZIP value of 97212. In making the match decision for character strings in a full item match, PFS:FILE uses the following rules:

1. Any spaces before the first character and after the last character are ignored. If you previously used TABS, for example, to enter information in records, you will have a space before each item value in the record file. This is normal and is ignored in making the match. The same is true if you use TABS instead of ENTER in creating your retrieval specification.

2. If multiple spaces appear in an item value, they are treated as a single space.

3. No distinction is made between upper- and lowercase letters. This is useful in address files with names, as names can be in upper- or lowercase letters or a combination of the two.

Suppose in the mailing list file created in Chapter 4 you wish to find the address for Tom Jones. From the **PFS:FILE** Main Menu, select function 4 (Search/Update), enter the file name (**B:PROSPECT.DAT**), and press F10. The retrieval form will then be displayed. On it enter

LASTNAME: **Jones**   FIRSTNAME: **Tom**

Leave all of the other item values blank.
The following records will not match the retrieval specification:

LASTNAME: **Jones, Jr.**   FIRSTNAME: **Tom**
LASTNAME: **Jones**   FIRSTNAME: **Mr. Tom**

Note: In this example, the index was based on LASTNAME, so although the FIRSTNAME was also entered, the search was still faster than if the user had only used the FIRSTNAME to search. Searching on partial matches is the slowest. You can try this as an exercise, but you will not notice the speed difference on this file with only a few names. The difference will only become apparent on larger files.

Partial Item Matches

The second type of retrieval, the partial item match, is useful if you do not remember how to spell the item name in the record you are trying to locate, or can remember only a part of the spelling. To initiate a partial item match, on the retrieval specification use two periods before or after the item value you are trying to match. You can also use the two periods to locate any records in which the item value is not blank. For example, suppose you are trying to find the address for Mr. Wiggenbottom and you do not remember exactly how to spell his last name. All of the following retrieval specifications would retrieve the record:

> LASTNAME: **..bottom**
> LASTNAME: **..BOTTOM**
> LASTNAME: **Wig..**
> LASTNAME: **Wig..bottom**
> LASTNAME: **..bott..**

You can compare the partial item match with the "wild-card" matches that you instruct your operating system to perform when you use asterisks with the DIR command; the ".." could be roughly compared with the asterisk in making DIR matches. With a retrieval screen displayed (function 4 from the Main Menu), enter **..bottom** and press F10. Did you get what you wanted?

Another way to do partial matches is to use the "@" character (the at-sign) to match any record with any character in the "@" position. For example, for Mr. Wiggenbottom the following retrieval specifications would also work:

> LASTNAME: **Wi@@enbo@@om**
> LASTNAME: **Wigg@nbottom**

The "@" is a wild-character match and can be used if you are not sure about one or more characters in the name. This type of match is roughly comparable to DIR matches using "?". Unlike the "..", the "@" is used on searches to match only individual characters: for each missing character, you must enter one "@". Try this type of retrieval using function 4 (Search/Update) from the Main Menu, and when the retrieval screen is displayed, enter **Wi@@enbo@@om** as the last name to retrieve your address.

A partial item match can also be used with character strings that are actually numbers. For example, all inventory items in the range 4300 to 4399 could be retrieved with the specification

PARTNO: 43@@

Of course, in this case you could also use "43.." to find the match.

Numeric Item and Range Matches

The third and fourth types of retrieval specification, the numeric item match and the numeric range match, can be used if the item value is numeric. PFS:FILE *always* stores the item value as a character string. If the character string is a number, however, you have the option of using the numeric item and numeric range matches. The difference between these two types of retrieval and the full and partial matches is in the rules that PFS:FILE uses to determine whether a match has occurred. The rules for numeric item and numeric range matches are as follows:

1. Any characters other than numerals, a hyphen, or a period are ignored.

2. A minus sign (hyphen) before the first digit or after the last digit will make the value negative. Multiple minus signs are ignored.

3. If there are multiple decimal points in the value, all but the first are ignored.

In a numeric *item* match, the logic symbols ">", "<", and "=" can be used. In the numeric *range* match, the ">" and "<" symbols *cannot* be used and instead the two dots (as in a partial item match) are used. The last example in the previous section ("PARTNO: 43@@") could have been done with a numeric range match instead of the method used.

For numeric item matches *or* numeric range matches, you must specify that you wish to treat the item value as a number by *beginning* your retrieval specification value with one of the following characters:

< > =

You then follow this signal character with a number if you are doing a numeric item match, or a numeric range if you are doing a numeric range match. Each of these characters signals to PFS:FILE that you wish to treat the item value as numeric. The equal sign is used to retrieve all records in which the value of the item matches the specified value; the "<" is used to find records with values less than the specified value; and the ">" is used to find records with values greater than the specified value. Remember that the "<" and ">" symbols can be used only for numeric *item* matches.

Under the rules for numeric matches, slashes and colons can be included in times and dates and are ignored for retrieval purposes. In addition, a dollar sign will be ignored. The following examples show the actual item value and how it is seen for numeric match purposes.

Actual Value	Type	Specification Value
$1,834.06	CURRENCY	1834.06
20:45	TIME	2045
84/04/14	DATE	840414

To retrieve on a numeric value, use the signal character "<", ">", or "=" and the value; for example, to find the record with a part number equal to 4299, use

PARTNO: =4299

Or to find all record items dated later than December 31, 1983—that is, on or after January 1, 1984—use the following specification:

DATE: >83/12/31

Remember that under the numeric match rules the slashes are ignored.

To gain experience with the numeric range match, select function 4 (Search/Update) from the Main Menu and try to retrieve all of your addresses with a ZIP code between 90000 and 98000. To do this, on the retrieval screen next to "ZIP:" enter:

=90000..98000

Don't forget to use the equal sign.

The NOT Match

The final type of match is the NOT match. The NOT match can be used with full item, partial item, numeric item, or numeric range matches to retrieve records that do *not* match the specified criteria. The retrieval specification is identical to a normal specification, except that it is preceded by a slash.

For practice, try to locate all prospects that do *not* end in "bottom." Assume Mr. Wiggenbottom has already been sent some advertising material and you wish to mail the same material to other prospects. Again use function 4 (Search/Update), press F10, and on the retrieval screen next to "LASTNAME:" enter:

LASTNAME: /..bottom

Notice that this time you will retrieve all of the prospects *except* Mr. Wiggenbottom.

USING THE RETRIEVAL SPECIFICATION

The retrieval specification is used to perform any of three operations on records: update them, remove them, and print them from PFS:FILE or PFS:REPORT. As an exercise, try a retrieval using function 4 (Search/ Update) from the Main Menu. When the function is initiated, the retrieval specification screen will be displayed (Figure 9-4). Now enter a retrieval specification to match any particular criterion in the stored file, such as

LASTNAME: /CHR..

This specification will retrieve all records except the record for Mary Christmas. Notice that the match is made whether uppercase or lower-case characters are entered.

After the specification is entered, press F10 to start the scan. The search starts with the most recent form entered and works backward, displaying each match on the screen. As each is displayed, you can review it, edit it, delete it, or print it by using the specified function key (Figure 9-5) shown at the bottom of the screen. If you have multiple

```
                         PROSPECTS

    LASTNAME: /CHR..              FIRSTNAME:

    ADDRESS:
    CITY:                  STATE:     ZIP:

    PHONE:

    NOTES:




    DATE:

    --------------------------------------------------------------------
    File: B:PROSPECTS.DAT          RETRIEVE SPEC            Page 1

    F5-Date     F6-Time                              F10-Continue
```

Figure 9-4. *Entering a retrieval specification*

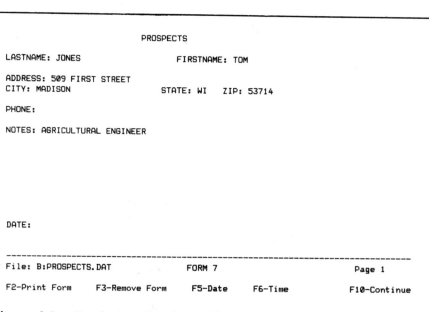

```
                         PROSPECTS

    LASTNAME: JONES               FIRSTNAME: TOM

    ADDRESS: 509 FIRST STREET
    CITY: MADISON            STATE: WI   ZIP: 53714

    PHONE:

    NOTES: AGRICULTURAL ENGINEER




    DATE:

    --------------------------------------------------------------------
    File: B:PROSPECTS.DAT          FORM 7                   Page 1

    F2-Print Form   F3-Remove Form   F5-Date   F6-Time      F10-Continue
```

Figure 9-5. *Retrieving the first address*

page forms, you can use the PGUP and PGDN keys to move between pages on a retrieved form. When you are finished, you can continue to the next match by pressing F10 again. After the entire file is scanned, the screen will display the number of matches that were found.

Practice different types of retrievals on your file until you understand each type of retrieval and how they differ from one another. Try at least one retrieval of each type. Notice the difference when the indexed item is used (LASTNAME) and when other items are used (you won't notice much on a small file) and, finally, when an indexed item and other items are used together in the retrieval specification.

REMOVING RECORDS FROM A FILE

If you wish to remove records from a file, select function **6** from the Main Menu (Remove) and enter the name of the file, **B:PROSPECT**, from which you wish to remove records. Be sure you have a copy of the file before starting. Use the necessary disk designator. Press F10, and you will see the retrieval specification form. Suppose, for example, we wish to remove the address for Mary Christmas from the file. Enter the specifications for the records you wish to remove (LASTNAME: **CHR..**), and press F10 again. You will then see the warning screen:

SELECTED FORMS ABOUT TO BE REMOVED

Press ESC to abandon this operation
Press F10 to continue

Press F10 and the removal process will begin. After the process is completed, you will see a screen displaying the number of records removed. Press F10 and you will be returned to the Main Menu.

EXTRACTIONS

There may be situations in which a file becomes too large for a disk and you wish to take part of the file and move it to a second disk. An example might be a mailing list file, which could start fairly small but eventually grows beyond the capability to store on a single disk. In this case you might wish to take some of the file (for example, all the Portland addresses) and move it to a second disk. After the extraction of the Portland addresses to a second disk, the selected addresses could be removed from the first disk. This process of moving selected records from one file to another is called *extraction*. To do extractions, you will use the Copy function. Like the merge process, extraction generally requires two disk drives or a hard disk drive. You should, of course, create a copy of your file with your records *before* starting an extraction.

To begin the extraction process, format a blank disk on which you can store the addresses you extract. The formatting procedure is described in your DOS manual. Start PFS:FILE, select function **3** (Copy), and enter the name of your source file that has now grown too large; remember to begin with any necessary disk designator. For this example, enter **A:PROSPECT.DAT** as the source file. Be sure to use the correct designator, because in this case you will copy records *from* Drive A *to* Drive B. For a two-drive system, remove the program disk and put your source ("from") disk in Drive A. Put your blank, formatted disk in Drive B. If you are using a hard disk, you should have room for both files on the hard disk and you will not need to use any drive designators. Press F10 when your disks are ready. You will then see the Copy Function Menu (Figure 9-1).

On the Copy Function Menu, select option **1** (Copy Design Only). Next to "NEW FILE NAME:" enter your destination file name with any necessary disk designator (such as **B:PORTLAND.DAT**), and then press F10. You should be careful *not* to use the name of the source file as the destination file. After you press F10, the form design *only* will be copied to your destination disk. After the form design is copied, you will be returned to the Main Menu.

Now select function **3** (Copy) a second time, and without changing the file name on the Main Menu (which is still **A:PROSPECT.DAT**), press F10. You will see the Copy Function Menu again. Enter the destination file name again, **B:PORTLAND.DAT**. This time, select option **2** (Copy Selected Forms). Press F10. The retrieval specification screen will then be displayed for your file. To specify the criteria for selecting records that are to be moved to the new file, TAB to one or more items and add the selection criteria. For example, TAB to the ZIP field and enter:

ZIP: **97212**

Press F10, and the desired records will be moved to the new file on Drive B. As each form is copied, it will be displayed on the screen. When the copy is completed, press F10 to return to the Main Menu. You could also have retrieved these same addresses by specifying the city as "PORTLAND" instead of specifying the ZIP.

You now have one last item to complete. The records copied to the second file are still in the original file. If the purpose was to make two smaller files from the original file, these copied records must be removed from the source file. In some cases you may wish to leave your extracted records in the source file. An example would be a mailing you wish to make to selected prospects in your file. You may wish to keep the whole file intact, but you plan to work with this subgroup for a while and need to sort, update, and manage it. You may wish, in this case, to leave the master file intact and work with your extracted file. The original file, of course, will not have any of the address changes that you make in your extracted file.

If you wish to remove the extracted records from the source file, select function **6** (Remove) from the Main Menu and enter your source file name, **B:PROSPECT.DAT**, with the source file on Drive B. Press F10 and you will see the retrieval specification form. Enter the specifications for the records you wish to remove (such as ZIP: **97212**), and press F10 again. You will then see the warning screen. Press F10, and the removal process will begin. After the process is completed and the Portland addresses are removed, you will see a screen displaying the number of records removed. Press F10 and you will be returned to the Main Menu.

In entering your retrieval specifications for file extractions or record removals, you can use full item matches, partial item matches, numeric matches, numeric range matches, or NOT matches. The general extraction procedure, in summary, is as follows:

1. Using the Copy Design Only option of the Copy Function Menu, copy an empty form design from an old file to a new formatted disk to use for the new file.

2. Choose the selection criteria using the Copy Selected Forms option of the Copy Function Menu.

3. Copy the selected forms to the new file by pressing F10.

4. If necessary, use the Remove function to remove the extracted records from the source file.

You cannot copy selected forms to an empty disk. The form must first be copied and a new file created on the disk; then the selected forms can be copied to the new file on the disk.

You can modify the form after step 1 if you wish, adding or deleting items of the record in the new form before copying the selected records. Of course, if you add a new item on the destination form, the value for this item is not in the old file and so you will have to add it manually using the Search/Update function after the copy is completed. If you delete items on the new form after the first step, that data cannot be transferred from the old file.

If you use function 2 on the Copy Function Menu more than once for the same destination file, each time you use it the selected addresses will be appended to any addresses already there. You can use this function as many times as necessary to add records from one or more files to the destination file. For example, on your first use of Copy you could select a certain ZIP code range. A second use of Copy could then add other records with another ZIP code range.

CHAPTER
TEN

Changing a File Design
With PFS:FILE

There will be occasions when you will need to redesign a form you have
already created. And it is very likely that if you delete one item from the
file, you will not wish to lose the information you have already stored in
the file for other items. With PFS:FILE, it is very easy to redesign a
form to include additional items or to eliminate items that were in a
previous form without losing information. Three common types of file
design change will be considered in this chapter.

- Changing a form for a file that does not contain records or data

- Changing single page forms for a file containing data

- Changing multiple page forms for files that contain data.

There are two notes of caution before starting: first, to change a file
design, you must have either two floppy disk drives or a hard disk drive.
The copy function requires a work area in which to create the copy —
the extra drive provides this work area. Second, if you change the name
of an item in the file, you will lose all of the information that has been
stored for the item. If you want that information, it must be reentered.

CHANGING FILES WITHOUT DATA

If you have not loaded any data to a file, changing the form is very easy. As an exercise in changing a file without data, you can recreate B:PROSPECT.DAT just as you created it in Chapter 4, and then put it on a blank disk. Do not put any data into this form. You could also start this next exercise by using the same disk that contains your PROSPECT.DAT file and creating a file with the same design and with a new name, such as "EXAMPLE.DAT". Refer again to Chapter 4 if you need help in creating this file.

As you create this form, deliberately make a mistake: do not put a colon after the ADDRESS item (see Figure 10-1). Now use PFS:FILE and try to add a record to this new file. As soon as you try to enter a record using Add, you will be alerted to your mistake. The highlighting tells you the colon is missing. To correct your mistake, return to the Main Menu by pressing ESC, select function 1 (Design File), and enter the file name that you used for this example: **B:PROSPECT.DAT**. Press F10. When the Design File Menu is displayed (Figure 10-2), select function 2 (Change Design) and press F10 again. You will see the blank form that you created earlier with the item name missing the colon. Use the

```
                         PROSPECTS

    LASTNAME:                    FIRSTNAME:


    ADDRESS
    CITY:                  STATE:     ZIP:

    PHONE:

    NOTES:






    DATE:

    ------------------------------------------------------------
    File: B:PROSPECT.DAT              DESIGN              Page 1

    F5-Date    F6-Time                              F10-Continue
```

Figure 10-1.   A file design with an error

```
DESIGN FILE MENU


1 - CREATE FILE

2  CHANGE DESIGN




SELECTION NUMBER: 2
```

F10-Continue

Figure 10-2.   *The Design File Menu*

CURSOR CONTROL keys to move the cursor to the correct place, and add the colon. Press F10, and the form has been redesigned. (See Figure 10-3.) Now try to add a record to this file. You will see the correct structure this time.

If you need to add an item or redo the layout of the form for aesthetic reasons and the file contains no records, changing the file is just as easy. Use the same Change Design function (function **2** of the Design File Menu) and display the form on the screen. Use the CURSOR CONTROL keys, SPACE BAR, INS, and DEL keys, and change the form as you wish. Since there is no data to be lost, no precautions are necessary. Before reading further in this chapter, you should create a simple form and then change it before adding any data.

CHANGING FILES THAT CONTAIN DATA

If the form contains only one page and the file already contains one or more records, PFS:FILE makes it very easy to change the form design. You will now see how this is done by changing the design of the file MODEMS.DAT, which already contains data. Before starting, however, be sure you have have taken two precautions. First, be sure you have created a copy of the old file. To create this copy, use the Copy function

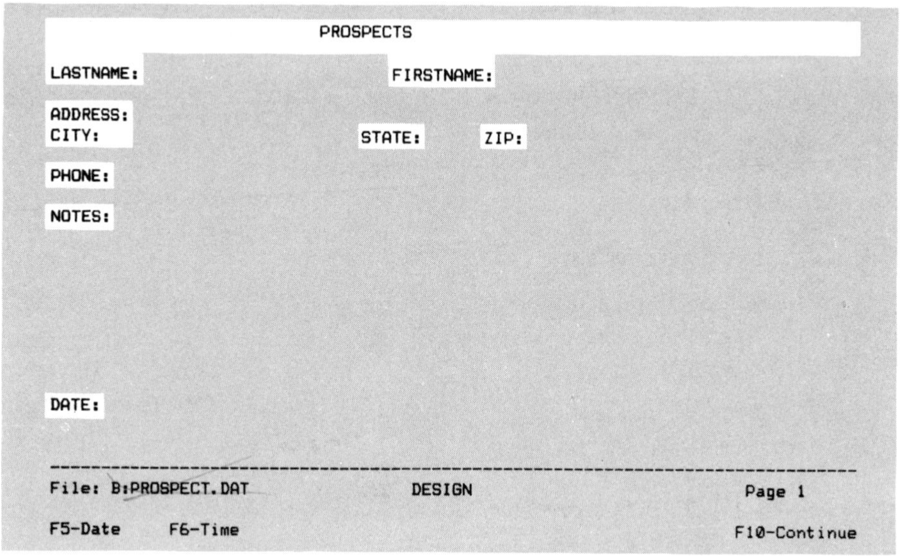

Figure 10-3.   *The corrected file*

(function 3) from the Main Menu. Enter **B:MODEMS.DAT** as the file name and press F10. The file name that you enter on the Copy Menu should, of course, be different from the original; for example, use the name **TEMP.BAK**. This copy is important in case the file should be inadvertently damaged during the redesign process.

Second, PFS:FILE needs work space to create the new file. Be sure the proper drive is assigned as the work drive. This work drive normally defaults to Drive B. If you wish to use a different drive for the work space or plan to use a hard disk that is not Drive B, you will need to use the SETUP program that came with PFS:FILE to change this work drive.

NOTE: The following steps need be completed only if the setup was not done at installation. If you are using a dual floppy system, the SETUP program will be on the same disk as PFS:FILE and can be started as shown:

A>**SETUP** ENTER

If you are using a hard disk, copy the SETUP program from the PFS:FILE disk to the hard disk and start the program as shown:

C>COPY A:SETUP.EXE C: ENTER
C>SETUP ENTER

When SETUP is started, it will tell you it can change the work drive and ask if you wish to escape. Pressing ESC will exit the program. If instead you press F10, the program will continue. You will see the SETUP options (see Figure 10-4). Change the work drive designation to the drive you wish using the TAB key to move about the menu. Use the F10 key to save the selection and return to the operating system. You only need to use SETUP to set the work drive the first time you want to redesign a file. After this, the program remembers what drive has been selected as the work drive, and you will need to use SETUP again only if you want to change the work drive assignment.

If you are using a floppy disk drive for the work drive, be sure a blank, formatted disk is in the drive and start PFS:FILE. As an example, use the form in Chapter 5 (B:MODEMS.DAT), which did not include any item for the modem protocol, for the modem listing. You have already entered several modems to the form and suddenly you discover your mistaken omission of the protocol item. How would you correct your mistake?

To begin, a copy of this file should have been made, the work drive

```
WORK DRIVE: B:


SERIAL PRINTER NAME: COM1:

BAUD RATE: 1200

PARITY( NONE, ODD, EVEN ): NONE

BYTE LENGTH( 7 OR 8 ): 8

NUMBER OF STOP BITS( 1 OR 2 ): 1




                                            F10-Continue
```

Figure 10-4. The Setup Menu

```
                         MODEM PRODUCTS

        COMPANY:

        MODEL:



        COMPUTER INTERFACE:
        TELEPHONE INTERFACE:
        SPEED:


        NOTES:




        LAST UPDATE:

        ----------------------------------------------------------------
        File: B:MODEMS.DAT              DESIGN                Page 1

        F5-Date      F6-Time                             F10-Continue
```

Figure 10-5.   Before the file design is changed

B: MODEMS-1

should be set correctly, and, if you are not using a hard disk, a blank disk should be in the work drive. If you have not created a copy or defined the work disk, do both steps before proceeding.

From the PFS:FILE Main Menu, enter option 1 (Design File), enter the file name **B:MODEMS.DAT**, press F10, and you will see the Design File Menu (see Figure 10-2). Select option 2 (Change Design) from this menu and press F10 again. The program will then warn you that the file will be changed and that there is a possibility of losing data (you will learn shortly *why* there is that possibility). Press F10 to continue. You will then see the blank form you created earlier (see Figure 10-5). But this time the item names are not highlighted. Use the CURSOR CONTROL keys to move the cursor down to the "NOTES:" line. Overtype this with

PROTOCOL:

Press ENTER, and then at the beginning of the next line type

NOTES:

```
                    MODEM PRODUCTS

        COMPANY:

        MODEL:


        COMPUTER INTERFACE:
        TELEPHONE INTERFACE:
        SPEED:


        PROTOCOL:
        NOTES:



        LAST UPDATE:

--------------------------------------------------------------------------------
        File: B:MODEMS.DAT              DESIGN                      Page 1

        F5-Date    F6-Time                                     F10-Continue
```

Figure 10-6. *After the file design is changed*

(See Figure 10-6.) Now press F10. You will see the program process each form, displaying it on the screen as it is processed. The time required for processing will depend on the size of the file. Notice that the order in which the forms will be processed is the opposite of the order in which they were entered; the last modem you entered will be processed first. After processing has been completed, you will be returned to the Main Menu.

You now have a new file. If you use Search/Update (function 4) on this file (which, if it is on a new disk, has the same name as the original file — MODEMS.DAT), you will see that all of the records are in this file and all of the items have the right value (including "NOTES:", the item that was moved) except for the new item, "PROTOCOL:". For each record in the file, you must enter the value for "PROTOCOL:". To enter the values of this new item, from the Main Menu enter function 4 (Search/Update) and the file name **B:MODEMS.DAT** and press F10. You will then see your empty new form and a request for retrieval specifications. Since you wish to update all forms, press F10. You will then see the last form displayed. TAB to the "PROTOCOL:" item and update the value of the new item with **103**, which is one type of standard used for modems. Press F10, and you will then see the next form

Table 10-1. *Input Modem Data*

MODEM PRODUCTS

MODEM PRODUCTS	PART	SPEED
ANCHOR AUTOMATION	MARK 1	110-300
	MARK 12	300-1200
	MARK II	110-300
	MARK III	300/1200
ANDERSON JACOBSON, INC	A242A	100-300+
BIZCOMP CORPORATION	1080	300
	PC:INTELLIMODEM	300/1200
HAYES MICROCOMPUTER PRODUCTS	1200b	110-1200
	SMARTMODEM 1200	110-1200
	SMARTMODEM 300	110/300+
MFJ ENTERPRISES	MFJ-1232	110/300
MICROPERIPHERAL CORPORATION	MICROMATION A1	300
	MICROMATION O1	300
NOVATION	212 APPLE CAT II	110-1200
	APPLE CAT II	300-1200
PRENTICE CORPORATION	POPCOM X100	300/1200
TANDY CORPORATION	DC-1200	300/1200
VEN-TEL, INC.	PC MODEM PLUS	110-1200

displayed. Continue in this way until you have entered the value of the new item for each form. For each record, type the protocol value **103** if the fastest speed is 300 or 300+, and **212** if the fastest speed is 1200. Use Table 10-1 as the source of your input data.

There are some limitations in changing forms with PFS:FILE. An important limitation is that the new form will contain information only for items that have the same item name in the old and new files. If, instead of moving an item, you *change the name* of the item, none of the information that appeared in the old file for that item will load to the new file with the new item name. You will have to enter all the information for that item on each form in the file. You should be careful, then, to change an item name only if it is necessary. This is the reason you get the warning message when you choose the Change Design function from the Design File Menu.

A related limitation is that if you move an item to a new location in the form, the value will still load to that item correctly, but only if you spell the item name *exactly* as before. If in moving an item on the form you misspell the name at the new location, you will lose all the information for that item: the information will not be loaded to the new file because the program cannot find an item name that corresponds. It also follows that if, in redesigning your file, you inadvertently leave an item out of the new file, you will lose all the information for that item in redesigning your file. This is why it is a good idea to always make backups before changing a file.

Notice that the method of changing the file design is essentially the same whether or not the file contains data. The only difference is that if the file does contain data, the copy must be made first, and a warning message is displayed before you initiate the redesign.

There will be times when, in redesigning a form, you inadvertently leave too little space for the old value for an item to fit on the new, redesigned form. For example, in redesigning a form you might leave less room for the last name, and a last name that used to fit on the form will no longer fit. If you attempt such a change during the redesign, the process will be interrupted and the screen will display a warning message. At this point you have one of three choices:

1. You can abort the entire redesign process with the old file intact.

2. You can edit the item value that does not fit the new form.

3. You can delete the displayed record and continue.

The next key you press will determine what will happen:

ESC Stop the entire transfer process. You will be returned to the Main Menu with the original file intact and no changes made.

F10 Continue. The old form will be displayed with the cursor positioned at the first character of the item value that will not fit the new form. You can then edit this item value and press F10 to continue.

F3 Delete this record from the file and continue.

CHANGING FILES
WITH MULTI-PAGE FORMS

With PFS:FILE you can change the design of multiple page forms by using the same procedure as with single page forms. The only difference is that you can change the design on only three pages at a time. (However, they need not be successive pages; you could change, say, pages 1, 3, and 7 in one step.) If you need to change more than three pages of a form, do two or more file design passes, changing only three pages at a time. For example, if a form has six pages and you are changing only three of them, you can change all three pages in one single redesign process.

If in changing the design of a multiple page form you move an item to a different page, PFS:FILE will nevertheless load the correct value to the item on its new page. When data is transferred during the redesign, PFS:FILE will first try to find the item on its original page. If it is not found there, the program will search through the pages consecutively, trying to find the item. It does not matter if the item is moved forward (to a later page) or backward (to an earlier page); if the item exists, PFS:FILE will find it and will load the information correctly.

As an exercise, modify the PROSPECT.DAT file so that you have more space for notes. Create a second page and move the "NOTES:" item to it. There are three steps in this modification:

1. Copy the old form design from the PROSPECT.DAT file to a new file.

2. Modify this old design (a one-page design) to a new, two-page design.

3. Move the data from the old file to the new file.

You will quickly see how easy this is. From the Main Menu, select function 3 (Copy), enter the old file name, **A:PROSPECT.DAT**, and press F10. On the Copy Function Menu select option 1 (Copy Design Only), enter the new file name, **B:PROSPECT.DAT**, and press F10. This will copy the design over and complete the first step. Now from the Main Menu select function 1 (Design File), enter the *new* file name, **B:PROSPECT.DAT**, and press F10. From the Design File Menu select option 1 (Change Design) and press F10. The old form design is now displayed. Use the CURSOR CONTROL keys to move the cursor to the "NOTES:" item and overtype this with spaces to remove the item from this page (Figure 10-7). Press the PGDN key and you will see the next

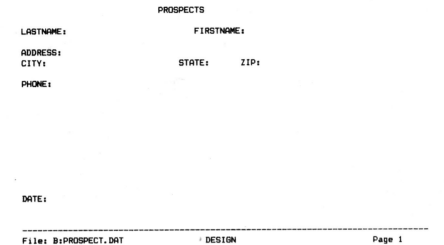

```
                       PROSPECTS

     LASTNAME:                     FIRSTNAME:

     ADDRESS:
     CITY:                STATE:      ZIP:

     PHONE:




     DATE:


     --------------------------------------------------------------------
     File: B:PROSPECT.DAT           DESIGN              Page 1

     F5-Date     F6-Time                                F10-Continue
```

Figure 10-7. *Changing the first page of the form*

```




     NOTES:














     --------------------------------------------------------------------
     File: B:PROSPECT.DAT           DESIGN              Page 2

     F5-Date     F6-Time                                F10-Continue
```

Figure 10-8. *Changing the second page of the form*

page of the form, which is now blank. Enter the item **NOTES:** at the top left of this page (Figure 10-8). Now press F10 to save your new form and return to the Main Menu.

The final step is to move the old data to this new form. Select function **3** (Copy) from the Main Menu, enter **B:PROSPECT.DAT** as the old file name, and press F10. On the Copy Function Menu select option **2** (Copy Selected Forms), enter the new file name, **B:PROSPECT.DAT**, and press F10. The retrieval form will be displayed. Press F10 again and all of the old data will be copied to the new form, including the values for "NOTES:". After completion, you can view your new file with function **4** (Search/Update) and the new file name, "**B:PROSPECT.DAT**". You will need to use the PGDN and PGUP keys to view both pages of each form.

PART
THREE

Advanced PFS Applications

CHAPTER
ELEVEN

Integrating
PFS Software

The PFS programs are designed to work together as integrated software. You can enter tabular reports that you create with PFS:REPORT into documents that you create with PFS:WRITE. You can do exactly the same thing with graphs that you create with PFS:GRAPH. Using PFS:WRITE and address files that you create with PFS:FILE, you can compile form letters that appear individualized. Using PFS:ACCESS, you can send documents that you create with PFS:WRITE to another computer. Figure 11-1 shows how the five PFS programs described in this book can be used in combination. In this chapter you will learn of useful ways in which you can integrate PFS programs.

When you prepare to use the PFS products together, one of the first steps you will take is to decide how to organize your disks and files. If necessary, review the appropriate sections in Chapters 1 and 5.

COMBINING REPORTS AND DOCUMENTS

One of the integrative tasks you are likely to perform frequently is adding a tabular report created with PFS:REPORT to a document created with PFS:WRITE. To include a tabular report, you must have

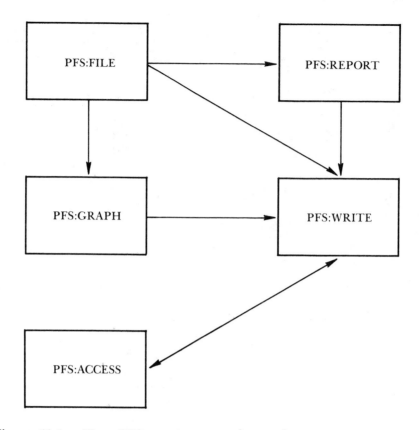

Figure 11-1. *How PFS programs work together*

written the report to a disk using **PFS:REPORT**. On the Report Option Menu of PFS:REPORT there is an option that enables the report to be printed to the disk instead of to a printer. This disk copy of the report will be in ASCII format. As an exercise, try this now, using your MODEMS.DAT file and the following procedure. (If you need help or review, refer to Chapter 5.)

Bring up PFS:REPORT and select function **1** (Print), press the TAB key, enter the file name **MODEMS.DAT**, and press F10. Skip the retrieval screen by pressing F10 and examine the Report Options Menu (see Figure 11-2) displayed next. Enter the title **MODEM DIRECTORY** and skip to the "OUTPUT TO:" option. Next to the "OUTPUT TO:" option you will see "lpt1:"; overtype it with **MODEMS.PRN**. Be sure to use a disk designator if necessary as in Figure 11-2. Press F10. On the

```
                    REPORT OPTIONS


      TITLE: MODEM DIRECTORY

      PRE-DEFINED REPORT NAME:


      OUTPUT TO: B:MODEMS.PRN

      LINES PER PAGE: 66        PAGE WIDTH: 80




                                        F10-continue
```

Figure 11-2.   *Report Options Menu*

specification screen displayed next, enter **1S** next to COMPANY and **2** next to MODEL. Press F10 again, and the report will be written to the disk. Exit PFS:REPORT by entering function 4 (Exit PFS:REPORT) and pressing F10.

Now bring up PFS:WRITE, select function 1 (Type/Edit), and press F10 to get a blank screen. Enter the following introductory text for your document:

April 3, 1984

John, here is the report you wanted. I hope it will meet
your needs.

The tabular report you created earlier with PFS:REPORT can be added to the end of this text by either of two methods: using the JOIN command or using the APPEND command.

The JOIN Command

The first method is to use the JOIN command described in Chapter 3. You *must* use the command with two asterisks, one before the command

and one following the file name, but you can abbreviate the command "J":

∗J B:MODEMS.PRN∗

Be sure to use the proper disk designator and put a space between it and the "J". After you have done this, return to the Main Menu by pressing ESC. Select function 3 (Print) and press F10 twice in succession to print the document. You do not need to enter the document name.

After the document is printed, return to the Main Menu (by pressing F10) and enter function 1 (Type/Edit). Then press F10 to return to your document. Notice that the tabular report is added at print time to the document. The report is never displayed on the screen. If you wish, you can also use the ∗N∗ command (NEW PAGE) before the JOIN command to force the report to start on a new page (see Chapter 3).

Each time the document is printed using the JOIN command, the document referenced must be on the disk drive specified. The document joined at print time (MODEMS.PRN) can be a PFS:WRITE document, a PFS:REPORT report, or a document from a non-PFS program. Graphs created with PFS:GRAPH cannot be added by the use of the JOIN command, but there is a way to integrate them into a document (described in the next section of this chapter).

A document cannot be joined to another if it already has a JOIN command within it, but multiple JOIN commands can be used to print a single document that is larger than can be stored in a computer's memory; for example:

∗J CHAPT1.DOC∗
∗N∗
∗J CHAPT2.DOC∗
∗N∗
∗J CHAPT3.DOC∗

The APPEND Command

There is a second method to add a report to your document: the APPEND command. With the same document displayed on the screen, try it by deleting the entire JOIN command line you added in the last exercise. Position the cursor at the end of the text, that is, below the last line. Now press F9 (Append). At the bottom of the screen a question is displayed:

NAME OF DOCUMENT TO APPEND:

Enter the file name **B:MODEMS.PRN** and press F10. Notice that this time the tabular report is *immediately* added to the document and can be viewed on the screen. Now you can press ESC to return to the Main Menu. Select function 3 (Print) and then press F10 twice to print the document.

Which of these two methods you elect to use will depend upon your application. In most cases, the JOIN command is better because it makes no increased demand on your disk storage space. By contrast, the use of F9 adds the report to the document, so the size of the file used to store the document on the disk is increased by the size of the report. With the JOIN command, the report is not stored as a part of the document, and so disk space is saved, no matter how many documents the report is combined with. The advantage of F9 is that you can see immediately on the screen what the document will look like. And in many cases the disadvantage just described may not apply unless the tabular report is needed for another document; the separate report file can be deleted after F9 has been used to join it to another document. Once it is part of the document, printing the document no longer requires referencing an external report file on the same disk. Everything you need is now a part of the document file. *Both* of these methods will work to enter almost any type of disk document to a PFS:WRITE document.

If the report file and the document file are on separate disks and you want to use the JOIN command to print the document and the report, the disk with the report file should be in the drive for the data disk when the document is printed. If, instead, you use the APPEND command (F9), the disk with the report file should be in the data disk drive when the F9 key is pressed. This may mean some disk swapping, as documents are being read or written to disk, because the disk with the document file must be in the drive when the document is being accessed or written. The document file is not used at print time because the document is printed from the computer memory.

You can also use JOIN and F9 (Append) to load documents created by PFS:WRITE even if they are in the special PFS:WRITE format. In fact, using F9 to retrieve a document is easier than using the Get function you have been using in exercises in previous chapters. Try this now by

```
                      DEFINE PAGE MENU




            LEFT MARGIN: 10      RIGHT MARGIN: 70

            TOP  MARGIN: 0       BOTTOM MARGIN: 0

            PAGE LENGTH: 66




    HEADING:

    FOOTING:



    F1-Help                                        F10-Continue
```

Figure 11-3. *Settings for printing a continuous form*

clearing the screen — press ESC, press 5 (Clear), and press F10 twice — and returning to the edit screen — enter function 1 (Type/Edit) and press F10. The edit screen should now be blank. Press F9 (APPEND), enter a document name, **B:TEST.LTR**, and press F10. The letter should now be displayed on the screen. If you wish, you can use the Print function to print the letter as in the first method.

If you are using PFS:WRITE to create a newsletter, you can get a continuous printout (no paging) that is useful for cutting and pasting by using the PFS:WRITE Define Page Menu to set the top and bottom margins to zero (see Figure 11-3).

PUTTING GRAPHS IN DOCUMENTS

Graphs created with PFS:GRAPH can be included as parts of documents, but only if two conditions are met: First, the graph must have been saved as a picture file (see Chapter 6). Second, you must have a graphic printer. If you have not done so already, return to PFS:GRAPH and, using the file name "SALES.PIC", create a PIC file of the sales data used as an example in Chapter 6.

Now return to PFS:WRITE, select function 1 (Type/Edit), and press

F10 to get the blank screen. Enter the following text as an example. Notice the graph command in the text:

April 5, 1984

Jack, in reviewing our sales for the past year, I notice an apparent seasonal jump in the early part of the year. Has this happened in previous years?

GRAPH B:SALES.PIC

Bill Smith

The first asterisk will determine where the file is printed on the page: the upper left edge of the graph will start at the asterisk. Be sure to use the proper disk drive designator. The GRAPH command can be abbreviated as "G" if you wish. To print this document, return to the PFS:WRITE Main Menu (by pressing ESC), select function **3** (Print), and press F10. On the Print Menu you will see the question whether you are using a graph created by PFS:GRAPH, to which you will need to answer **Y**:

JOINING PFS:GRAPH (Y/N):Y

Press F10. You will then see a Printer Selection Menu. Graphs can be printed only with graphic printers, and when you initiate the print that includes a graphic output, a special Printer Selection Menu will be displayed from which you can select your printer (see Appendix B for the list of printers). Select your printer from the displayed list and press F10 again. The document will now print. If the SALES.PIC file is not on the current data disk, the printer will stop when it gets to the point where the graph is supposed to go and will ask you to load the disk with the SALES.PIC file. Put the disk with that file in Drive B and press F10 to continue. The graph will be automatically inserted into a space approximately 3 1/2 × 4 1/2 inches, occupying 18 lines of a page. If the graph will not fit on the current page, PFS:WRITE will skip to the next page and start the graph on that page. Plan your text so that the graph is printed on the desired page. Any number of graphs can be added to a document. The graphs are not stored as part of the document, and each time the document is printed, the PIC files needed for the document must be on the disk in the drive referenced in the document (for example, Drive B in "*GRAPH B:SALES.PIC*").

PRINTING FORM LETTERS

You can use PFS:WRITE to create letters that incorporate addresses or any other type of information supplied from files created with PFS:FILE. Thus, using address files created by PFS:FILE, you can print a single form letter (which is called a template) to make any number of individualized letters. There are three steps in the printing of form letters:

1. Creating the data in a PFS:FILE file that will individualize the letters.

2. Creating the template letter.

3. Printing the final letters.

For example, in Chapter 4 you created an address file of prospects that might be interested in a new product. Assuming this is the PROS-PECT.DAT file, you have, then, already completed the first step of the process—using PFS:FILE to create the file that contains the personalized information.

The second step is to use PFS:WRITE to create the *template* letter that will be used with the addresses. For this example, bring up PFS:WRITE, from the Main Menu select function 1 (Type/Edit) and press F10. When the edit screen is displayed, enter the letter shown in Figure 11-4, the template letter.

```
April 3, 1984

*FIRST NAME* *LAST NAME*
*ADDRESS*
*CITY*, *STATE*  *ZIP*

Dear *FIRST NAME*,

Thank you for your inquiry on our products.  Enclosed you
will find information on the specific products in which you
expressed an interest.  If you have further questions, please
do not hesitate to contact me directly.

Sincerely,


Bill Smith, Marketing Manager
```

Figure 11-4. *The template letter*

```
                    PRINT MENU

          FROM PAGE: 1   TO PAGE: 1

          PRINT TO: LPT1:

          PAUSE BETWEEN PAGES (Y/N): N

          NUMBER OF COPIES: 1

          SINGLE/DOUBLE/ENVELOPE (S/D/E): S

          INDENT: 0

          JOINING PFS:GRAPH (Y/N): N

          PFS FILE NAME: B:PROSPECT.DAT
```

F1-Help   F10-Continue

Figure 11-5.   *The Print Menu for printing a form letter*

The template letter is a master letter that contains the information that will be in all the letters and contains, as well, codes or variables used to represent values that will be added later from a file created by PFS:FILE. Notice in the figure that each variable is set off from the text by two asterisks, one preceding the variable and one following it. You can insert punctuation and spaces between the variables, and these will appear in the printout. You can use a name other than the one in the item in PFS:FILE, and the variable name is not printed when the letter is printed—only the substituted value from PFS:FILE.

The third step is the actual printing of the letter. Press ESC in PFS:WRITE to return to the Main Menu, select function **3** (Print), and then press F10. You will then see the Print Menu displayed (Figure 11-5). If you want the printer to pause between each letter so you can load letterhead paper, locate the "PAUSE BETWEEN PAGES" query and enter **Y**. Enter the file name **PROSPECT.DAT** on the option "PFS FILE NAME", supplying any necessary disk designator. At this point, if your address data file is on a different disk from the one currently in the designated drive, you will need to change disks and put the data disk in the drive. The program disk should now be in Drive A and your disk with the addresses in Drive B. When the data disk is ready, press F10. You will then see the Retrieval Specification form displayed as in Figure 11-6. At this point, you can select the portion of the file to use for the

```
                               PROSPECTS

      LASTNAME:             FIRSTNAME:

      ADDRESS:
      CITY: PORTLAND        STATE:            ZIP:

      PHONE:

      NOTES:




      DATE:


      ---------------------------------------------------------------------
      File: B:PROSPECT.DAT            RETRIEVE SPEC           Page  1

                                                         F10-Continue
```

Figure 11-6.   *The Retrieval Specifications screen*

form letter. In this case, move the cursor to "CITY:" by pressing the TAB key and enter PORTLAND, since you wish the letter sent only to prospects in that city. Press F10. You will then see the identifier screen displayed. This looks much like the Retrieval Specification screen (Figure 11-6) except that the phrase "IDENTIFIER SPEC" appears at the bottom of the screen. This screen permits you to match the labels you used in the template letter with the item names in the record file. In this case, enter **LAST NAME** for LASTNAME, press the TAB key once, and enter **FIRST NAME** for FIRSTNAME. Since all the rest of the items have the same name when used in the template letter, press F10 twice and your form letters will begin to print. If you requested it on the Print Options Menu, the printer will pause between each letter, permitting you to insert letterhead stationery. The letter, when printed, will appear as in Figure 11-7.

There are a few other options that may be of use to you when you are printing form letters. If you wish, you can insert information from a PFS:FILE file into the actual body of the letter. Use the double asterisks and the file item name, or make up your own name and match it to the file item name with the identifier specification form, as you just did in the example inserting names and addresses. If text is inserted in the

```
April 3, 1984

MARY CHRISTMAS
234 FOX ROAD
PORTLAND, OR  97212

Dear MARY,

Thank you for your inquiry on our products.  Enclosed you
will find information on the specific products in which you
expressed an interest.  If you have further questions, please
do not hesitate to contact me directly.

Sincerely,



Bill Smith, Marketing Manager
```

Figure 11-7.   *The individualized form letter*

body of the letter, a "T" should be used with it to force the wordwrap to work at print time; for example:

Here is the enclosed information on *PRODUCT (T)* that you requested.

You can also, if you wish, use an "R" (instead of the "T") to force the entry to right-justify on the right asterisk. This is used for inserting numeric entries and aligning decimal points.

PRINTING REPORTS WITH CALCULATED VALUES

Sometimes you may wish to print a report that contains information that is not in a file but can be calculated from information in a file. There are basically two types of reports with calculated information. The first is a report in which totals, subtotals, counts, or averages are calculated from information in a column already in the file. For example, you might have a file of students' grades from which you could calculate the class average at the end of the report. In the second type of report, calculations are performed on values in existing columns to

```
SCORE:


STUDENT:
```

```
--------------------------------------------------------------------------------
File: B:SCORE.DAT                    DESIGN                          Page 1

F5-Date      F6-Time                                            F10-Continue
```

Figure 11-8.   *File for student scores*

create an entirely new column. For example, you might have an inventory report in which the total value of each part in the inventory (calculated as quantity on hand times cost) is *not* kept in the files as an item but can be supplied, by calculation, during printing. You will see details of both types of reports in this section. Of course, you may wish to combine the two types; the second example will show how this is done.

To see an example of the first type of report, create a file that could be used to keep student grades on a test. Using PFS:FILE, select function 1 (Design File) on the Main Menu, enter the file name as **B:SCORE.DAT**, and press F10. From the Design File Menu select option 1 (Create File) and press F10. Create the file shown in Figure 11-8 with the item names **STUDENT** and **SCORE**. Return to the Main Menu by pressing F10. Now select function 2 (Add), press F10, and add the student names and grades shown in Figure 11-9. Enter each name exactly as shown with the last name first. Press F10 to store each record after entry. After the last student name and grade have been entered and the next blank form is displayed, press ESC to return to the Main Menu. From there enter function 7 (Exit PFS:FILE) to leave PFS:FILE.

Now bring up **PFS:REPORT** and from the Main Menu select func-

```
                    HISTORY TEST 1

               STUDENT            SCORE
               ----------------   -----

          ALGOOD, JOSEPH           73
          HILL, JOYCE              78
          LAWRENCE, SANDY          96
          LEEDON, SUSAN            88
          LOVEJOY, BILL            86
          TINKER, BILL             94
          WHITE, SHERRY            92
          WRIGHT, JIM              81

                                -------------
                            Average:    86
                                -------------
```

Figure 11-9.   *The student score listing with average*

tion 1 (Print a Report). When the Report Options Menu is displayed, enter the report title as **HISTORY TEST 1** and press F10. The report specification screen is then displayed. Fill this out as shown in Figure 11-10. The "2A" next to "SCORE" means that the scores are to be printed in the second column ("2") and the average ("A") at the bottom of the column. The "1" next to "STUDENT" indicates that the student names will be printed in column 1. Since column 1 is used for sorting

```
SCORE: 2A

STUDENT: 1
```

```
------------------------------------------------------------------------
File: B:SCORE.DAT              REPORT SPEC                       Page 1

F7-Derived Columns                                          F10-continue
```

Figure 11-10.   *Report specification for student scores*

Table 11-1.   Codes Used for Column Calculations

T	Total. Value will be treated numerically, and all of the values in the column will be totaled with the total printed at the end of the report.
ST	Subtotal. Produces a subtotal for each new value in column 1 and grand total at the end.
A	Average. Values are treated as numeric values and an average is printed at the end of the report.
SA	Subaverage. A subaverage is calculated and printed for each new item in column 1. Column average is printed at the end of the report.
C	Count. This counts and prints the number of values in a column.
SC	Subcount. Prints a subcount for each new item in column 1, with a complete count at the end.

purposes, the listing will be alphabetical by student name. Press F10 to print the report. The final report will look like the list that is shown in Figure 11-9.

Table 11-1 presents a list of codes that can be used as commands to force (that is, require calculation of) totals, subtotals, counts, and averages on existing columns. When you use these commands, PFS:RE-PORT automatically assumes that the column information is numeric. If any of your values is a zero, it is important when you are forcing counts and averages that you enter a zero instead of leaving a blank for that value. If you leave the item value blank when entering the record, the record will not be used in a count or average calculation, and the result you get will be incorrect.

Several good uses for this first type of calculated report are sales reports showing total sales by salesperson, salary reports showing salary totals by department, and sales summaries showing average sales per salesperson.

The second type of calculated report is one in which a column of information is created by calculation from information in the file. This new column is called a *derived column.* As mentioned earlier, an inventory report is the most general application of this type of calculated report. In this application, you would not want to store the value of the total quantity of each part in stock as an item, since it could always be calculated when needed.

An inventory file generally contains the part number, a part description, the quantity of each part on hand (QOH) and the price of the part (both wholesale and retail prices may be included). To print a report of the total inventory value, you would need to know the total inventory value of each part in the inventory. For each part in the inventory, the quantity on hand is multiplied by the cost; this calculation creates an extended cost.

This calculated value is never kept in the file. It is calculated "on the fly" as the report is printed. Up to three derived columns can be created in a single report. (The derived columns are counted as a part of the total of sixteen columns you are permitted in a report.)

Try making an inventory file using PFS:FILE to experiment with derived column calculations. From the PFS:FILE Main Menu select function 1 (Design File), enter the file name **B:INVENT.DAT**, and press F10. On the Design File Menu select option 1 (Design File) and press F10. Create the file shown in Figure 11-11. This shows the part number, description, quantity on hand, and a single price. Press F10 to return to the Main Menu, select function **2** (Add), and press F10. Add about ten part numbers to this simple file using the data in Figure 11-12. When entering the prices, you can omit the leading zeros.

Now create a report showing the total inventory value. Using

```
NO:
DESCRIPTION:
QOH:
PRICE:
```

```
File: B:INVENT.DAT              DESIGN                  Page 1

F5-Date     F6-Time                              F10-Continue
```

Figure 11-11.   Inventory file design

```
                        INVENTORY LISTING

            NO            DESCRIPTION          QOH     PRICE
           -----    ---------------------      ---     -----
           1142     HUB GREASE COVER            23     0.35
           2113     MASTER RETAINING ROD         3     2.43
           3412     RIM FASTENING SCREW         43     0.09
           5129     REMOVABLE FENDER             2    14.87
```

Figure 11-12. *Inventory listing*

PFS:REPORT call up function 1 (Print a Report) to print the entire report and press F10. Press F10 to retrieve every record in the file. On the Report Options Menu, enter **INVENTORY LISTING** as the report heading, and then press F10 again. The Report Specification screen will be displayed next. Fill this out as shown in Figure 11-13. The numbers you enter assign each item to a column in the printed report. The "N" stipulates that the value will be printed as a numeric value and the decimal points, if any, will be aligned. Before pressing F10, press F7 and you will see the "DERIVED COLUMNS" screen (Figure 11-14). Notice that three columns can be entered from this screen, the maximum number of derived columns permitted. In this example, you will use only one. For the heading, enter **EXT COST**. Enter the formula #3*#4,

```
     NO: 1
     DESCRIPTION: 2
     QOH: 3N
     PRICE: 4N
```

```
     -------------------------------------------------------------------
     File: B:INVENT.DAT              REPORT SPEC                 Page 1

     F7-Derived Columns                                       F10-continue
```

Figure 11-13. *Inventory Report Specifications*

```
                        DERIVED COLUMNS



         HEADING: EXT COST
         FORMULA: #3*#4
         REPORT SPEC: 5T



         HEADING:
         FORMULA:
         REPORT SPEC:



         HEADING:
         FORMULA:
         REPORT SPEC:
         ----------------------------------------------------------------------
         File: B:INVENT.DAT              REPORT SPEC

         F7-Return to Form                                         F10-continue
```

Figure 11-14.   *Inventory derived columns screen*

which means that in this column the value of column 3 (Quantity on Hand) times column 4 (PRICE) should be printed. You identify each column number by entering a pound sign (#) in front of it. For the specification "REPORT SPEC:" enter **5T**, which will print the extended cost in column 5 and a grand total of the column at the end of the report. Press F7 again to return to the specification screen and then press F10. This will print the total value of the inventory at the end. The final report printout is shown in Figure 11-15.

```
                        INVENTORY VALUE

         NO        DESCRIPTION         QOH     PRICE     EXT COST
         ----      ----------------    ---     -----     --------
         1142    HUB GREASE COVER        23     0.35         8.05
         2113    MASTER RETAINING ROD     3     2.43         7.29
         3412    RIM FASTENING SCREW     43     0.09         3.87
         5129    REMOVABLE FENDER         2    14.87        29.74

                                                       -----------
                                              Total:        48.95
                                                       -----------
```

Figure 11-15.   *Inventory report showing total value*

In your formulas, you can use constants and column numbers with the normal operators "+", "−", "∗" (multiply), and "/" (divide). You can also use parentheses.

REPORTS USING KEYWORDS

Another type of report that can be created with PFS:REPORT is used when items are stored against keywords and retrieved by keywords. An example might be a quotation file. Each quotation record will contain the author, a reference, and the quotation with one or more keywords. A *keyword* is one or more descriptive words that could be used to retrieve the record. To create this file, use PFS:FILE and from the Main Menu select function 1 (Design File). Enter the file name **B:QUOTE.DAT** and press F10. From the Design File Menu select option 1 (Design File) and press F10 again. Create the form shown in Figure 11-16. Now press F10 to return to the Main Menu, select function 2 (Add), and press F10 again. Add the records shown in Table 11-2. Notice that you will add only three records (quotations). Two of the records each have two keywords. In adding these two records, enter the two keywords for each, separated by one space. Thus, for the quotation that begins "Money is merely...,"

```
KEY:
AUTHOR:
SOURCE:
TEXT:
```

```
File: B:QUOTE.DAT              DESIGN                    Page 1

F5-Date      F6-Time                                 F10-Continue
```

Figure 11-16.   *Quotation file design*

Table 11-2.   *Quotation File Report*

QUOTATION FILE

KEY	AUTHOR	TEXT
COMMUNICATIONS	MARTIN, JAMES	Once we are able to have messages delivered almost instantaneously, the way we utilize them changes completely.
ECONOMICS	MARTIN, JAMES	Money is merely information, and as such can reside in computer storages with payments consisting of data transfers between one machine and another.
FUTURE	SCHAAR, JOHN	The future is not a result of choices among alternative paths offered by the present, but a place that is created, first in mind and will, created next in activity. The paths to it are not found but made, and the activity of making them changes both the maker and destination.
INFORMATION	MARTIN, JAMES	Once we are able to have messages delivered almost instantaneously, the way we utilize them changes completely. Money is merely information, and as such can reside in computer storages with payments consisting of data transfers between one machine and another.

the key value is "ECONOMICS INFORMATION." When you add your records, use single words for each key, separating the words by spaces (see Figure 11-17). If you have a two-word key, omit the space between the two words. Any number of keywords can be used for the "KEY:" item.

When you use PFS:REPORT to create the report, the "KEY:" part *must* be defined as the first column. Start PFS:REPORT as usual, selecting function 1 (Print a Report) and pressing F10. Press F10 again to print

```
KEY: ECONOMICS INFORMATION
AUTHOR: MARTIN, JAMES
SOURCE: THE WIRED SOCIETY
TEXT: Money is merely information, and as such
can reside in computer storages with payments
consisting of data transfers between one
machine and another.
```

```
---------------------------------------------------------------------------
File: B:QUOTE.DAT                    FORM 3                    Page 1

F2-Print Form      F3-Remove Form      F5-Date      F6-Time      F10-Continue
```

Figure 11-17. *Entering the quotation*

all the records, and on the Report Options Menu enter the title as **QUOTATION FILE**, set the page width to **132**, and press F10. You will need to have wide paper in your printer or have the printer set for compressed print. When the Report Specification screen is displayed, enter **1K** for the key value (Figure 11-18). Enter the remaining values as shown and press F10. The report will be printed in keyword order, and each record will be listed one time for each keyword (Table 11-2). Experiment with this in an application before putting too many records in a file. Since PFS:REPORT does not justify the text, how the text is entered controls how it is displayed on the report.

The keyword feature is very powerful. With it you can create everything from bibliography files with abstracts to address files of people by interests, and article files that are keyword-coded.

PRINTING GRAPHS FROM FILES

You can also use PFS:GRAPH to print graphs from files created with PFS:FILE. In Chapter 6 you created a graph with PFS:GRAPH by entering the data manually. In this section you will enter the data to a file created with PFS:FILE, and then use this file to print a graph with PFS:GRAPH.

```
KEY: 1K
AUTHOR: 2
SOURCE: 3
TEXT: 4
```

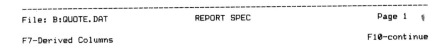

```
----------------------------------------------------------------------
File: B:QUOTE.DAT              REPORT SPEC                 Page 1  ¶

F7-Derived Columns                              F10-continue
```

Figure 11-18. *Quotation File Report Specification*

You must first create the file. From the PFS:FILE Main Menu select function 1 (Design File), enter the file name **B:FILEGRPH.DAT**, and press F10. On the Design File Menu select option 1 (Create File) and press F10. Design the file shown in Figure 11-19 for the data you will use for the graph. After the design is completed, press F10.

From the Main Menu select function 2 (Add) and press F10. Add the following data. For the MONTH item, do not enter the name of the month; enter only its number.

MONTH	SALES
1	2576
2	1252
3	2742
4	1843
5	2420

When the next screen is displayed for the sixth record, enter ESC to return to the Main Menu. Start PFS:GRAPH, from the Main Menu select function 1 (Get/Edit Data), and press F10. On the Get/Edit Data Menu, select option 3 (Get PFS:FILE), select graph **A**, leave the "MERGE (Y/N):" at the default value of "N", and then next to

```
                       PRODUCT A
    MONTH:
    SALES:




    ----------------------------------------------------------------------------
    File: B:FILEGRPH.DAT              DESIGN                    Page 1

    F5-Date    F6-Time                                      F10-Continue
```

Figure 11-19.   *The file for PFS:GRAPH input*

"DIRECTORY OR FILE NAME:" enter **B:FILEGRPH.DAT**. The Retrieval Specification screen will then be displayed. Press F10 to retrieve all of the records. A blank form will then be displayed for the graph specifications.

On the graph specifications you must enter the X Data Format and the X data. Next to "MONTH:" enter **X--I** to indicate that an identifier format should be used for the X axis. Next to "SALES" enter **Y**. Press F10 again to begin reading the data. After the data is read use function **2** (Define Chart) to define the graph (see Chapter 6) and then function **5** to print it. The printed graph should look like Figure 11-20.

Before leaving this section, continue to experiment with the data you created and print other graphs. Learn how to use the "Copy" function in PFS:FILE to reorder the data to get the desired graph. Try other X Data Formats, such as "X--D," to display the data.

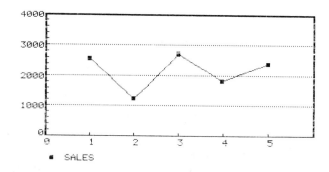

Figure 11-20.   *The graph*

CHAPTER
TWELVE

Using PFS Software
With Other Systems

There will be occasions when you would like to merge PFS files, graphs, and documents with data produced on software products other than PFS programs. For example, you might want to use a document created earlier with another word processor, like WordStar, as part of a PFS:WRITE document. In this chapter such applications are described in detail.

READING FOREIGN FILES WITH PFS:WRITE

Most word processors, PFS:WRITE included, store documents in a special format that is not readable by other word processors. For example, word processors employ special codes to distinguish between carriage returns created by the word processor (*soft* carriage returns) and carriage returns entered from the keyboard (*hard* carriage returns). Other special codes that may be used by the word processor in the output text include codes for boldface printing and other print enhancements as well as other types of control notations. There is no standard for these special characters that the various word processors use, and the codes vary between products. PFS:WRITE can read *only* files with standard ASCII characters, that is, only alphabetic, numeric, and punctuation characters that have been defined as a part of the standard ASCII character set.

Even though word processors store most documents in a special form with their own special codes and formats, most word processors make provisions for transferring files from the word processor to other programs. In order for documents to be transferred between various word processing programs and utilities, the word processor must provide a means of writing the document to the disk as a "print image." This means the disk file image looks exactly like the printed paper copy. Most word processors will take out any special characters (such as those initiating print enhancements) in printing the document to disk, so the disk file image contains only standard ASCII characters. WordStar, Select, and almost all word processors have this provision. PFS:WRITE, like other word processing products, can also print a document to a disk file.

PFS:WRITE can read any of these disk print image files from other word processors to create a PFS:WRITE file, or can incorporate a document created by another word processor into a document created by PFS:WRITE. This can be done in any of three ways. For the sake of simplicity, call the document being read into PFS:WRITE from another program (another word processor, a communications program, or any text processing utility) the *foreign document*.

The first method can be used if you want the foreign document to create another document in PFS:WRITE. This method will clear the work area in PFS:WRITE before starting, so it cannot be used to add the foreign document to a document you have already created. To experiment with this, be sure you have some type of foreign document on your data disk. This can be any type of ASCII file (text information) created by any editor or word processor. Use the COPY command in the operating system, if necessary, to copy this file to your data disk. Start PFS:WRITE, select function 4 (Get/Save/Remove), and press F10. When the Get/Save/Remove Menu is displayed, select option 1 (Get Document), enter the name of your foreign document, remembering also to supply the disk designator, and press F10. In using this first method, whatever margins currently exist in the foreign document will remain and can be viewed on the screen after the document is loaded. For example, if the foreign document has a left margin of 15 spaces, when the document is loaded you will see each line starting 15 spaces from the left edge. The margins on the ruler line, however, will remain at a left margin of 1 and a right margin of 78. If you use the Define Page Menu you will see the 1 and 78 values. The reason for this is that PFS:WRITE stores the margin information as a header in its own PFS:WRITE files. The foreign document file does not have this header, and the margins default to 1 and 78. The old margin spacing in the foreign document is converted to spaces in the new PFS:WRITE document.

The second and third methods permit you to append or add the foreign document to a file already created by PFS:WRITE. In the second method, the file created with PFS:FILE is first loaded to the work area and the cursor is moved to the location where you wish to add the foreign document. To try this method, clear your work area in PFS:FILE if necessary by selecting function **5** (Clear) and pressing F10 (you may have to press it twice). Now from the Main Menu select function **1** (Type/Edit) and press F10. You should now see a blank edit screen. Press the F9 key (Append) and you will see the prompt for the file name:

NAME OF DOCUMENT TO APPEND:

Enter the name of the document to append and press F10. The foreign document file will then be read and appended to your document (added at the cursor location). Since you did not start with any text in the work area, the foreign document is all that will be displayed. Your PFS:WRITE margins will remain at the left margin of 10 and a right margin of 70. If the foreign document has margins in the print image, they will be added to these PFS:WRITE margins. For this reason, if you plan to use this method, you should create the foreign document with *no* margins. With most word processors, this is done by creating the foreign document using the "non-document" mode (option "N" with WordStar, "A" with Select). Otherwise, the new text will not be aligned with your PFS:WRITE text.

The third method is to use the JOIN command, which will include the foreign document at print time as

J TEMP.PRN

This method is similar to the adding of documents and reports using the JOIN command, as described in Chapters 3 and 11. In this case, any margin space in the foreign document will be preserved and *not* added to any current PFS:WRITE margin. The text is added in a way similar to what happens when the GET command is used, except that existing PFS:WRITE margin settings are ignored and only the margins in the foreign document are used.

You can also use PFS:WRITE to edit or print files received by a communications program over a telephone line. Most communications programs do not save files in any special format. Any of these three methods can be used to retrieve and print a file of standard characters received with a communications program (see Chapter 7).

PFS:WRITE WITH dBASE II, FILE MANAGERS, AND REPORT GENERATORS

Files created with PFS:FILE cannot be read by dBASE II programs, and dBASE II files cannot be read by PFS programs. There is, however, one exception. You can include a report created with dBASE II in a document created with PFS:WRITE. To do this, use the ALTERNATE switch in dBASE II to create a text file within dBASE II; for example:

SET ALTERNATE TO REPORT.PRN

Now create a disk image of your report by printing to a disk file as

SET ALTERNATE ON
? 'THIS WILL BE PRINTED TO A DISK FILE'
SET ALTERNATE OFF

Use the ALTERNATE switch around any print statements that print the report, and the printed report will also be saved in a disk image. Any type of output (including display information) between the SET ALTERNATE switches will be in the disk file. Once the report image is created, use the PFS:WRITE program and the GET, F9, or JOIN command to create your PFS:WRITE document with the dBASE II report image (see Chapter 3). As a general rule, in creating the report from dBASE II, you should use a right margin of 60 so that the margins will be aligned with the rest of your PFS:WRITE document.

Of course, dBASE II is not the only program that can generate reports for your PFS:WRITE documents. Most file management programs can create reports with disk file images. If the program will write a report to a disk in standard ASCII format, you can use the report with PFS:WRITE documents.

Data created with **PFS:FILE** cannot be used directly with other file management programs, and **PFS:FILE** cannot use data created with other programs. The reason is that **PFS:FILE** has an extensive free-form capability that is implemented by storing data in a very compact format. The format does not interface well with the formats used by fixed-format file management software like that used by dBASEII, Condor, Knowledge Man, and other information management software.

PFS:FILE can create a document in standard ASCII format. This can be done by printing the output (such as mailing labels) to the disk. To do this, start a print as you would normally (using function **5** on the PFS:FILE Main Menu), and when the Report Options Menu is displayed, use the TAB key to move to the "PRINT TO:" option and enter the file name for the output. This will print an ASCII file that has one item on each line and as many lines for each record as the page length defined on the same Report Options Menu. For example, at 66 lines per page and a label of four lines per address, you would see 62 blank lines between any two records in the ASCII file. This cannot be read by dBASE II in this form, but could be converted by a BASIC program to a file form that could be read by dBASE II.

USING PFS:GRAPH
WITH SPREADSHEET SOFTWARE

Many manufacturers of spreadsheet software include the capability of saving the spreadsheet information in a DIF (Data Interchange Format) file. DIF is a special format that specifically enables data to be moved between programs of various manufacturers. At the present time, many spreadsheet products, Lotus 1-2-3 and VisiCalc among them, are capable of creating these DIF files. You can create a spreadsheet with one of these products, save the spreadsheet as a DIF file, and then send this DIF file to PFS:GRAPH to create a graph that could be part of a presentation.

You cannot *create* DIF files with PFS:GRAPH, PFS:FILE, or PFS:REPORT. PFS:GRAPH is the only PFS program that accepts DIF files. You can, of course, use data from a PFS:FILE to create a graph. As

	JAN	FEB	MAR	APR	YEARLY SALES STATISTICS MAY	JUNE
George Everson	4120	5123	4185	6124	5180	5155
Bill Fox	3124	4078	4098	5550	5774	4195
Jane Erickson	1024	4309	4378	5987	5298	6124
Total	8268	13510	12661	17661	16252	15474

Figure 12-1. *The starting spreadsheet*

an example of creating a graph from a DIF file, you will create a spreadsheet with Lotus 1-2-3, save it as a DIF file, and then graph this data with PFS:GRAPH.

First, you create the spreadsheet and then save it as a normal Lotus file. Lotus 1-2-3 normally saves a file that has a "WKS" extension. Figure 12-1 is an example of a spreadsheet created with Lotus 1-2-3 that will be used to create a graph with PFS:GRAPH. Titles, text, and unneeded rows and columns should be removed before saving the file in Lotus 1-2-3. Save only the information you will use for the graph or graphs (see Figure 12-2). Once you have created the WKS file, exit 1-2-3 to the Lotus Access Manager and select the Translate function. Use this function to translate the WKS file to a DIF file. You are now ready to use PFS:GRAPH.

Start the PFS:GRAPH program, select function **1** (Get/Edit Data) from the Main Menu, and press F10. When the Get/Edit Data Menu is displayed (see Figure 12-3), select option **2** (Get VisiCalc File). This option is used for VisiCalc, Lotus 1-2-3, or any DIF input file. Press the TAB key to move the cursor to the GRAPH query and enter **A**. Press the TAB key again to move the cursor to the file name query and enter the file name with any needed disk designator and an extension of DIF.

You will then see the Get VisiCalc Menu displayed (Figure 12-4). This menu is used to specify the format for the X data and the rows (or

JAN	FEB	MAR	APR	MAY
4120	5123	4185	6124	5180
3124	4078	4098	5550	5774
1024	4309	4378	5987	5298
8268	13510	12661	17661	16252

Figure 12-2. *Preparing the spreadsheet*

```
GET/EDIT DATA MENU


1   ENTER/EDIT DATA

2   GET VISICALC FILE

3   GET PFS FILE

  SELECTION NUMBER: 2

  GRAPH (A/B/C/D): A

  MERGE (Y/N): N

  DIRECTORY OR FILE NAME: B:PFS4.DIF



                                         F10-Continue
```

Figure 12-3. Getting the input data

columns) that will contain the X and Y data. The three queries on this menu should be answered using the following rules:

X   DATA. The number of the row or column of the spreadsheet from which to get the X data. Enter **1** .

Y   DATA. The number of the row or column of the spreadsheet for the Y data. Enter **2** for February data.

X   DATA FORMAT. Enter **I**, **N**, or **D** to define the format as identifier, numeric, or date format and the necessary identifiers if date format is chosen (see Chapter 6). In this example, enter **I**. Do not enter **1** or numeric values.

Press F10, and the data should then load to PFS:GRAPH. After the data has loaded, a message screen will be displayed:

5 Data Points Read

Press F10 to continue

Press F10 again and you will be returned to the Main Menu. You can then use function **5** (Print Chart) and press F10 to print the chart. You

```
                    GET VISICALC FILE MENU




                         X DATA: 1

                         Y DATA: 2

                         X DATA FORMAT: I




--------------------------------------------------------------------

FILE NAME: B:PFS4.DIF                                    GRAPH A
                                                       F10-Continue
```

Figure 12-4. *The VisiCalc Menu*

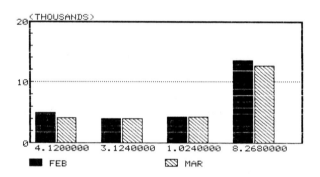

Figure 12-5. *The first graph*

```
X DATA FORMAT: I

                  X DATA                              Y DATA
     EVERSOLE                          5123
     FOX                               4078
     ERICKSON                          4309
     TOTAL                             13510




--------------------------------------------------------------------

GRAPH A                    ENTER/EDIT DATA                   PAGE 1
                                                         F10-Continue
```

Figure 12-6. *Editing the data*

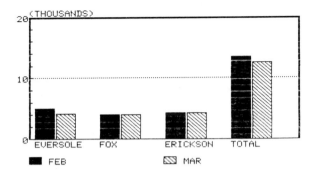

Figure 12-7. *The final graph*

can also load a graph "B" from the same DIF file, select graph "B" on the Get/Edit Data Menu, and select "3" (for March) as the Y Data. All other values are the same. The chart of these two graphs is shown in Figure 12-5.

To correct the labels, use function 1 again (Get/Edit Data) and press F10. From this menu, select option 1 (Enter/Edit Data) *instead* of the option 2 selected earlier. Select graph "A" and do *not* enter a file name. Edit the X data to the correct names (see Figure 12-6). You will need to do this for *both* files. Then print the chart again (see Figure 12-7).

You can use this method to create a wide variety of charts from the DIF file. If the X value is found more than once, the values will be added for the corresponding Y value. Data reduction will also be done if the MERGE option is selected. You will also notice from this example that how the rows and columns are defined in the spreadsheet is important. This, to some extent, controls the graphs. In some cases, you may wish to reverse the rows and columns before saving the spreadsheet.

WRITING FILES FOR NON-PFS PROGRAMS

You may sometimes wish to write a document with PFS:WRITE to be read by a non-PFS program such as a communications program or word processor. In this case, you will need to print your document to the disk with PFS:WRITE, since the internal PFS:WRITE file cannot be read by other programs. To print this file to the disk so that a document can be transferred to another program, start PFS:WRITE, select function 4 (Get/Save/Remove), and then press F10. When the menu for

```
                        PRINT MENU

          FROM PAGE: 1   TO PAGE: 1

          PRINT TO: B:TEST.PRN

          PAUSE BETWEEN PAGES (Y/N): N

          NUMBER OF COPIES: 1

          SINGLE/DOUBLE/ENVELOPE (S/D/E): S

          INDENT: 0

          JOINING PFS:GRAPH (Y/N): N

          PFS FILE NAME:



F1-Help                                            F10-Continue
```

Figure 12-8. *Printing a document to a disk*

Get/Save/Remove is displayed, select option 1 (Get Document), enter the file name **B:TEST.LTR** (note the use of the appropriate disk designator), and press F10. You will then see your letter displayed. Press ESC to return to the Main Menu, select function 3 (Print), and press F10. On the Print Options Menu use the TAB key to move the cursor to the "PRINT TO:" query. Enter the file name you wish for the print image. Be sure to use the necessary disk designator (see Figure 12-8). Use a standard extension (such as "PRN") for all of your disk file images. There should be no print enhancements in the file, and if you plan to edit or alter the file with another word processor or utility, you should use a non-document mode to read the file. For example, with WordStar you would read the PFS:WRITE document file using the "N" (non-document) option. With the Select word processor, you should set the ALTER mode from the Select Main Menu and then read the PFS:WRITE file. There will be a hard carriage return at the end of every line; so unless these were deleted, do not expect any other word processor to justify the text created by PFS:WRITE.

SPELLING AND GRAMMAR CHECKERS

Although Software Publishing now sells its own spelling checker, you may want to use a spelling checker you already have or a grammar checker to proofread the documents created with PFS:WRITE. Most of the wide variety of products on the market for this purpose can be used—if the utility does not put any special codes in the output file and leaves the characters as standard ASCII characters. Most word processors (PFS:WRITE among them) save text internally in a special code that is not standard ASCII characters. For this reason, the normal output of **PFS:WRITE** cannot be used as the input to a spelling or grammar checker. You can, however, print your **PFS:WRITE** document to a disk and then use this print image as the input to a spelling or grammar checker. Random House Proofreader, from Wang Electronic Publishing and Digital Marketing, is one such product that can be used with **PFS:WRITE** using the method now described.

If you have such a foreign spelling checker, you can use this example to practice spelling correction. As a first step you must create a document file with a spelling error. Start **PFS:WRITE**, from the Main Menu select function 4 (Get/Save/Remove), and press F10. Select option 1 (Get Document) from the Get/ Save/Remove Menu, enter the file name **B:TEST.LTR**, and press F10 to retrieve your test letter. Using the CURSOR CONTROL keys, move the cursor to the "o" in the word "Enclosed" in the last paragraph and press the DEL key three times to change the spelling to "Encld." Now press ESC to return to the Main Menu. This document must now be printed to the disk without the default margins. From the Main Menu, select function 2 (Define Page) and press F10. On the Define Page Menu enter 1 for the left margin, press the TAB key once, and enter **78** for the right margin. Press F10 to return to the Main Menu. The margins should now be altered. To save your document, select function 4 (Get/Save/Remove) from the Main Menu and press F10. Select option 2 (Save Document) from the Get/ Save/Remove Menu and enter the file name **B:TEST1.DOC**. Press F10 to save the document. Print the document to the disk by selecting function 3 (PRINT) from the Main Menu and pressing F10. When the Print Options Menu is displayed, press the TAB key twice to move the cursor to the "PRINT TO:" option. Enter the file name **B:TEST1.PRN** as the output file name and press F10. The document will then be printed to the disk. As a general rule, there should be no print enhancements in this draft copy. Add them later, after the spelling has been corrected.

After the file is printed to the disk, leave PFS:WRITE by using function 6 (Exit) on the Main Menu and use your spelling or grammar utility to scan the file for errors. Make your corrections from within the spelling correction utility. Now return to PFS:WRITE and retrieve this corrected document. To do this, select function 4 (Get/Save/Remove) and press F10. When the Get/Save/Remove Menu is displayed, select option 1 (Get Document) and enter the file name **B:TEST1.PRN**. Press F10. When the document is displayed, press ESC to exit to the Main Menu so you can set the correct margins. Select function 2 (Define Page) and press F10. When the Define Page Menu is displayed, enter **10** for the left margin. Press the TAB key once and enter **70** for the right margin. Press F10 to return to the document. The text should now be all aligned and the spelling corrected. Use ESC to return to the Main Menu and enter function 3 (Print). Press F10 twice to print the document. To save the new document after printing, select function 4 (Get/Save/Remove) from the Main Menu. Press F10, and when the Get/Save/Remove Menu is displayed, select option 2 (Save Document) and enter the new document name as **TEST2.LTR**. Press F10 and the document will be saved.

BEYOND PFS

By now it should be evident that the PFS programs described in this book are excellent for many applications and users, particularly for those who find the computer a new experience. Some of the advantages of the programs are

- They are easy to learn
- They are easy to use
- They have excellent documentation
- They are low in cost.

The day will come for many, however, when they will need features beyond the range of the PFS programs. This section looks at some of the limitations of four of the products and suggests directions for those who need features that PFS lacks.

PFS:WRITE enables the user to see the document as a collection of pages. In reality, the document should be more accurately viewed as a single entity. The create/edit process, formatting, and printing are all distinct operations performed on a single document. If a word processor is designed with this in mind, the formatting and printing commands can be much more extensive. Almost all other word processors on the market, for example, have right justification, which permits the user to align the right margin. PFS:WRITE does not. Most processors permit the user to change margins and other formatting features at any place in the document. PFS:WRITE does not. Printing features are also limited.

You cannot, for example, print at 12 characters per inch. You will also find that the special format of the PFS:WRITE files makes it cumbersome to interface the files with other utilities. The more complex word processors such as WordStar, Select, and Microsoft Word, although more difficult than PFS:WRITE to learn and use, all have these extended features.

PFS:FILE and PFS:REPORT are excellent file managers, permitting the user to build files and manage information in simple applications. Each, however, operates only with a single file at a time. You will also find that these have limited flexibility. You cannot write programs to manage the files or create special reports that use data from multiple files. The Quotation File example mentioned in Chapter 11 using keywords is cumbersome to use and report formatting is difficult. Most file management applications use at least two files at a time, and many require three or more. The LEDGER system that will be discussed in Chapter 13, for example, is an interesting approach to using a single file to create a general ledger system. For many applications, however, you would need at least three files for an adequate general ledger system. You will also have difficulty moving information in PFS:FILE to other programs, and you do not have much control over the output format of screens or reports—you can only create the input form. If you need more features and find the PFS products limited, you will probably find dBASE II the most popular product for most applications. To use it, though, you need to know something about programming.

PFS:ACCESS is excellent for simple access to the information utilities and the PAMS. But it has very limited file transfer capability, and you cannot use it to transfer programs as binary data between computers with error checking. It will also not work in an answer mode in which others can call into your system. Only log-on procedures can be stored, and if you have a collection of commands you are using frequently (called "macros"), you will have to enter these each time. This means using your utility instruction book frequently while you are on-line using expensive time. For information utility usage, one of the best programs is probably Smartcom II from Hayes Microcomputer Products, Inc. For file transfers, a popular program is Crosstalk XVI from Microstuf. These cost a little more than PFS:ACCESS and are a little more difficult to use.

Finally, many new integrated products, such as Framework and Symphony, offer tools for several applications in a single program. These are more difficult to use and learn than the PFS programs, but offer many extended features that are not available in the PFS programs.

Using **PFS SOLUTIONS** Programs

Often you can save both time and money by having someone else design the file forms and reports. Software Publishing produces more than a dozen prepackaged file and report designs for various applications. These products, each marketed individually as a component of PFS SOLUTIONS, can be purchased at a very nominal cost, about $20 each. They make it easy to begin using PFS software immediately without the need to design files or reports. Each product includes a form design and from three to seven report designs.

You will need to have PFS:FILE and PFS:REPORT to use any of these. Each of the PFS SOLUTIONS is easy to use and comes with the clear instructions that are characteristic of Software Publishing products. Each system includes records and report specifications you can view and use to print sample reports. After you gain experience with the data, you can remove the sample resources from the file and add your own resources. You might even want to purchase a few PFS SOLUTIONS products for the tutorial experience, since the packages give excellent examples of how to build files and reports. Table 13-1 lists twelve of the products and identifies the type of application for which

Table 13-1. PFS SOLUTIONS *Summary*

Product	Application
MAIL LIST	Manages mailing lists and telephone numbers.
CHECKS	Keeps a record of your banking transactions as well as invoice and purchase order information. Indicates outstanding payables at any time.
EMPLOYEE	Organizes and maintains vital information about employees—benefit entitlements, salaries, social security numbers, and birthdays.
TICKLER	Maintains ticker file, appointment schedule, and travel expenses.
INVENTORY	Monitors stock on hand and calculates profit margin.
INVOICES	This is a general-purpose invoice form that is useful for billing customers. Reports include tax summary, customer analysis, sales history, and purchase order register.
LEDGER	This is a general-purpose ledger with a chart of accounts and journal.
PAYROLL	Tracks withholding and other payroll information for employees through the year. Calculates W-2 information for each employee and overtime earnings for salaried and hourly employees.
HOME BUDGET	Tracks personal bank and credit card transactions. Includes bank checkbook reconciliation.
HOME INVENTORY	Tracks personal property, asset records, and valuable documents. Useful for supporting insurance claims.
STOCKS	Analyzes your stock portfolio. Includes realized and unrealized gains and losses, effective growth rates, and dividend yields. Reports show share location, agent, and commissions.
DISK LIBRARY	Manages your computer disk library, even printing the disk labels.

each is intended. Table 13-2 describes the reports for each product. One additional product not listed is the school recordkeeper. Higher in cost, it includes a collection of forms and reports applicable to a wide variety of needs in the educational environment. In this chapter three of these products are examined to see precisely how they work. Even if you plan to create your own forms and you feel that this chapter may not be applicable to your needs, you should read it through anyway, since it presents some valuable ideas about using PFS products.

Table 13-2. *PFS SOLUTIONS Report Overview*

Checks

Check Register

Payments to Other Parties

Invoice Register

Deposits and Other Items

Account Allocations

Disk Library

Diskette Labels

Software and Hardware Expenses

Disk Library by Type of Program

Disk Library by File ID Number

Service and Vendor Information

Serial Numbers, Warranty
Information

Employee

Benefits Checklist

Employee Telephone Directory

Departmental Salary Review

Employee Birthdays

Employee Mailing Labels

Home Budget

Bank Reconciliation Checklist

Fixed and Varying Expenses

Itemized Tax Deductions

Expenditures by Budget Category

Home Inventory

Assets by Location

Review Tickler for Valuable
  Documents

Asset Values and Appraisal
  Information

Warranty Information

Invoices

Sales Tax Collected

Customer Purchases

Purchase Order Register

Invoice History

Cash Receipts and Receivables

Mail List

Name and Address List

Telephone Directory

Company Telephone Directory

Mailing Labels

Ledger

Chart of Accounts

Account Closings

General Journal

Stocks

Current Stock Portfolio

Current Portfolio Values

Unrealized Gains and Losses

Realized Profits and Losses

Rank by Effective Growth Rate

Performance vs. Dow Jones

Relative Performance vs. Other Indexes

Tickler

Tickler Report

Appointment Schedule

Expense Log

Table 13-2.   *PFS SOLUTIONS Report Overview (continued)*

Inventory	Payroll
Price and Item Number List	Employee W-2 Calculations
Product Profit Margins	Net Pay Calculations
Purchase Register	Hourly Pay Calculations
Supplier Register	Payroll Taxes Payable
	Employee Payroll Stub

MAIL LIST

MAIL LIST can be used to keep track of names and addresses for mass mailings, prospect lists, or news releases. The file form includes space for the first and last names, company, address, ZIP code, three contact phone numbers (home, work, and one auxiliary), title, and comments. Included also are report forms that enable you to print a phone listing of home, work, and one auxiliary phone number; a phone listing alphabetized by company name that also shows names and phone extensions of company personnel, and an address report showing names and addresses. Mailing labels can be printed from MAIL LIST only by use of PFS:FILE. PFS:REPORT cannot be used for labels.

MAIL LIST includes one disk with a single file called MAILLIST. This is a data file for the addresses in a PFS:FILE format. The report specifications are stored as a part of this file. You will need both PFS:FILE and PFS:REPORT to use the file effectively. Seven sample records are already stored in the file. The disk can be copied—and indeed the first thing you should do when you buy any of the PFS SOLUTIONS packages is to create a copy. If you are using a hard disk, you will want to copy the file on the PFS SOLUTIONS disk to your hard disk.

After you have a copy of the file, bring up PFS:FILE and work with the copy so that you do not damage your original disk. *Do not use PFS:FILE with your original PFS SOLUTIONS disk.* Use the Search/Update function (function 4) of PFS:FILE to scan the records that are already in the MAILLIST file, studying the form design *and* how the data is loaded. This will show you how to enter data to the form.

After you have gained some familiarity with the form, exit **PFS:FILE** and bring up **PFS:REPORT**. Use the Print function (function 1), press F10 to start the print cycle, and print each of the predefined reports. Press F10 when the retrieval screen is displayed; and when the Report Options Menu is displayed, enter a title and the print specification name before pressing F10 again. On MAIL LIST, the pre-defined reports are called **PHONE, COMPANY,** and **ADDRESS**. For starters, print one of the first two reports. You can also use function **2** (Pre-define a Report) in PFS:REPORT to examine each of these pre-defined reports and see how they are set up. When you use this function, the names of all pre-defined reports are displayed with a request to enter a report specification name. Enter the name of the specification you wish to view and press F10. You can print the report specification by using function 2 (Pre-define a Report) on the PFS:REPORT Main Menu, displaying the report specification, and using the SHIFT and PRT SC keys to print the displayed screen to the printer. You can do the same with the file design by displaying the retrieval screen (using function 1 on PFS:REPORT) and using the SHIFT and PRT SC keys.

Now use **PFS:REPORT** and function 1 (Print) to print the remaining two reports. When you print the pre-defined ADDRESS report, you will get a message that the report is too wide. To print this report, exit **PFS:REPORT** and set your printer to compressed print (17 characters per inch). You can do this with most systems using a simple **BASIC** program. For example, for an Okidata 93 the following BASIC program will set the printer to compressed print:

```
10 LPRINT CHR$(27);CHR$(48)
20 LPRINT CHR$(29)
30 SYSTEM
```

You can also set the printer to compressed print by installing the PFS:REPORT program to send the necessary codes to the printer each time the PFS:REPORT program is started. Instructions for this are in Appendix D of the **PFS:REPORT** manual.

Once the printer is set to compressed print, reenter **PFS:REPORT** and on the Report Options Menu (from function 1) set the page width to **132**. The ADDRESS report will now print.

Before starting to add your own records, remove the sample records already in the file. Since you still have the master MAIL LIST disk, it is not necessary to save your file of this copy before removing the records. Use the PFS:FILE function **6** (Remove), and when the Retrieve Specification screen is displayed, press F10 to remove all records in the file. The file will now be empty and ready to receive your additions.

Study the design of the form and the report specifications and plan any changes you may wish. Either the form or the report specifications may be altered to your particular needs. You can even alter these at a later time or add new report specifications. If you wish to change the file design, use function **1** (Design File) from PFS:FILE, press F10, and select option **2** (Change Design) on the Design File Menu. Report specifications can be changed by using function **2** (Pre-define a Report) on the **PFS:REPORT** Main Menu and entering the name of the report specification you wish to change.

Once the form has been designed to meet your needs (or left without changes), begin the entry of your data using function **2** (Add) from the **PFS:FILE** Main Menu. Notice that if you use the same form design, you will not begin with Form 1. PFS:FILE does not reuse old form numbers when records are removed. You will start with Form 8.

In entering your data, standardize your rules and document these rules. Typical rules should include the following:

1. Standardize any entries for items which you may later plan to sort so that the entries will sort correctly. For example, if the entire name is treated as one item, *all* names should be entered in as lastname/firstname so that the sort will work correctly.

2. Use standard abbreviations and codes and use them consistently. For example, always use the same abbreviation for any given state, preferably approved by the U.S. Postal Service.

3. Eliminate unnecessary punctuation and use punctuation consistently. For example, decide whether or not you will use a period after "Mr".

4. Make all numeric entries the same length to ensure correct sorting. For example, ZIP codes should include all leading zeros.

5. Dates should be entered in YY/MM/DD order to ensure correct sorting.

As a final precaution, be sure you make backups of your data after every entry session.

TICKLER

Tickler files are used to schedule future events that must occur at a particular time. These include calls that must be made on certain days, reservations that must be made or confirmed for flights or lodging, reports that are due at particular times, and other routine jobs that can be scheduled in advance. The **PFS SOLUTIONS TICKLER** system can be used to manage tickler files and appointments and also to track business expenses. Although each of these is a separate function, they all use the same file.

TICKLER includes one disk with a single file called TICKLER. This is the master file for ticklers, appointments, and business expenses; three report specifications are stored as part of the file. You will need both PFS:FILE and PFS:REPORT to use the TICKLER system. Several sample records are already stored in the file. The disk can be copied, so the first thing you should do is to create a copy of the disk; or if you are using a hard disk, copy the file to it.

After you have created a copy, use function 4 (Search/Update) of PFS:FILE to scan the records that are already in the file. Study the methods for entering records and the items that are used. This will give you an idea of how to add your own data to the form later.

After you have gained some familiarity with the form, leave **PFS:FILE** and bring up PFS:REPORT. Use the Print function (function 1) and press F10. Select to print all of the records by pressing F10 on the retrieval screen. When the Report Options Menu is displayed, enter the title and the report specification name. With TICKLER, the valid predefined report names are APPOINT (for appointments), TICKLER (for ticklers), and EXPENSE (for expenses).

- The APPOINT report lists daily appointments in chronological order.

- The TICKLER report lists tickler items in chronological order.

- The EXPENSE report is a log of travel, meals, and other business expenses.

For the moment, print only appointments or the tickler file. You can also use function 2 (Pre-define a Report) on the **PFS:REPORT** Main Menu to examine any pre-defined report. All of the names of the pre-defined reports are displayed, and it is only necessary to enter the name of the report specification you wish to view from this list.

If you try to print the EXPENSE report, you will get a message that the report is too wide. Exit PFS:REPORT and set your printer to compressed print (17 characters per inch) and then try to print the report again, setting the page width to **132** on the Report Option screen when the printing is started.

Once you have printed all the reports, you may wish to print the form design or report specifications. As with MAIL LIST, you can use the SHIFT and PRT SC keys to print either of these. Refer to the previous section, on MAIL LIST, to see how this is done.

Before starting to add your own records, remove the sample records already in the file. It is not necessary to save the file, since you should still have the master disk. Use the PFS:FILE function **6** (Remove) and when the Retrieve Specification screen is displayed press F10 to remove all records in the file. At this point you can change the form or report specifications, if necessary, to meet any particular needs you might have.

Once the file is empty (except for the design information) and the design meets your needs, begin entering your own records using function **2** (Add) on the PFS:FILE Main Menu. Use the rules for standardization already described in MAIL LIST. Be sure to make backups periodically.

LEDGER

The PFS SOLUTIONS LEDGER system can be used by professionals and small businesses to manage business transactions. Charts of accounts, journal entries, account closings, and income statement information are all stored in a single file. Using appropriate report specifications, you can print simple general ledger reports from this file.

LEDGER includes one disk with a single file called LEDGER. The file also includes three report specifications that are stored as a part of the system. You will also need both PFS:FILE and PFS:REPORT to use the LEDGER system. Several sample entries are already stored in the file. The disk can be copied, so the first thing you should do is to create a copy of the disk, or if you are using a hard disk, copy the file to it.

After you have created a copy, use function **4** (Search/Update) of PFS:FILE to scan the records that are already in the file. Study the methods for entering the records and the items that are used. This will show you how to add your data to the form later. You might wish to print a copy of the file using function **5** (Print) from the **PFS:FILE** menu. Notice that the **BEGINNING BALANCE** item of each record is used to store the final account balance for each account.

After you have gained some familiarity with the form, leave **PFS:FILE** and bring up **PFS:REPORT**. Use the Print function (function **1**) and press F10 to print all of the reports. Initiate the printing of all of the records by pressing F10 while the Retrieval Specification screen is on display. When the Report Option Menu is displayed, enter the title and the report specification name. With **LEDGER**, the valid pre-defined report names are **CHART**, **JOURNAL**, and **CLOSING**.

- The **CHART** report is a listing of the chart of accounts and the description of each account.

- The **JOURNAL** report shows each entry and indicates if the ledger is in balance.

- The **CLOSING** report is used to report each balance sheet and income statement account.

For the moment, print only the chart of accounts using the **CHART** pre-defined report. You can also use function **2** (Pre-define a Report) on the **PFS:REPORT** Main Menu to examine how each of the reports is defined. After selecting function **2**, press F10. The pre-defined report names are displayed, and it is only necessary to enter the name of the report specification you wish to view from this list.

If you try to print the **JOURNAL** or **CLOSING** report, you will get a message that the report is too wide. Exit **PFS:REPORT** and set your printer to compressed print (17 characters per inch) and then try to print the reports again, setting the page width to **132** on the Report Option Menu when the printing is started.

Once you have printed all the reports, you may wish to print the form design or report specifications. As with **MAIL LIST**, you can use the SHIFT and PRT SC keys to print either of these.

Before starting to add your own records, remove the sample records that are already in the file. The master disk that came with the **LEDGER** should be kept separately with the original records intact. Use the **PFS:FILE** function **6** (Remove) and press F10. When the Retrieval Specification screen is displayed, press F10 to remove all records in the file. After all the records are removed, you can change the form or report specifications, if necessary, to meet any particular needs you might have.

Once the file is empty (except for the design information) and the design meets your needs, begin entering your own entries using function **2** (Add) on the **PFS:FILE** menu. Use the rules for standardization already described in the section on MAIL LIST. Be sure to make backups periodically.

APPENDIX
A

Useful Terms

access   To dial up, through a computer and modem, and successfully log on (gain admission) to an information utility, public access message system, or communications service.

ASCII text file   A file that contains only printable characters: alphabetic letters, numerals, and punctuation marks. The ASCII (an acronym for American Standard Code for Information Interchange) code is a standard means of storing character data and of exchanging messages and documents.

backup   A copy of some or all of the information on a disk kept in case the original is lost or damaged.

baud   A unit of measure (commonly bits per second) of the transmission speed in electronic communications. An alphabetic character is transmitted as either seven or eight bits.

BBS   Bulletin board system. See PAMS.

bit   The smallest unit of information in a computer's memory or operating system.

boot   To start a computer's operating system.

bulletin board   A community message system or PAMS.

byte   A unit of storage in a computer, composed of one or more bits; normally defines the storage required for a single character of text.

CBBS   Computerized bulletin board system. See PAMS.

"COM1:"   The first device driver in the IBM PC or XT for a modem or serial printer.

"COM2:"   The second device driver in an IBM PC or XT for a modem or serial printer.

command   A keystroke or input that assigns the computer a task.

connect time   The elapsed time since an electronic communications service was logged on to.

cursor   The symbol on the screen that indicates where the next action will occur.

data disk   The disk to which you write information (as opposed to PFS program disks, to which, for their protection, you should not write).

default value   The value used for a particular setting if the user does not alter the value. For example, the default value for the DOS device on all PFS products is a parallel printer connected to "LPT1:". The user can alter the default value to meet specific system needs.

device driver   The software used to send information to or receive information from an external peripheral such as a printer, modem, or terminal.

directory   A location on the disk that stores information about the names, locations, and sizes of the files on the disk. Also called the root directory.

disk   A removable magnetic recording medium used to store information. Disks can be used to store programs or data (information used by programs). Also called a diskette.

disk drive   A device that reads and writes on a magnetic disk.

diskette   See disk.

document   Any type of writing viewed as a collected whole. In the PFS context, each document is stored as a file.

DOS   An acronym for Disk Operating System, which refers to the PC DOS operating system used by the IBM PC and XT or the MS DOS used by IBM-compatible machines.

duplex   Refers to the transmission mode of communications hardware and software. Full duplex applies to the capability of simultaneously receiving and transmitting information. Half duplex applies to the capability of only sending *or* receiving information at any one time.

electronic communications   The transfer of information by means of computers and telephone lines.

electronic mail   The ability to send and receive messages to and from another computer.

extraction   Removal of part of a file to start a new file with the part removed.

file   A collection of information stored on a disk under a single name. A file in PFS:FILE, PFS:REPORT, and PFS:GRAPH is a collection of records of the same type along with the form used to create the individual records in the file.

foreign document   A non-PFS document.

form   A combination of items displayed in a particular order and used to add records to a file. The PFS manuals call both records and forms by the same name — forms.

format   (1) to prepare a disk to store data by storing certain timing marks and codes on the disk; (2) to organize text in a particular way for display or printout.

full duplex   See duplex.

function   A selection from a PFS menu that initiates a procedure.

function keys   Keys F1 through F10 on the IBM PC keyboard, used to perform certain specific tasks (see Figure 1-1 and Appendix E).

half duplex   See duplex.

hard disk   A magnetic recording device permanently installed in the computer for the storage of information. The hard disk, unlike the floppy disk, is not flexible and can store a large amount of information. A hard disk has faster disk access than a disk drive.

item   One piece of information in a PFS record (also called a field by some manufacturers). Records are composed of one or more items. A record for a part in an inventory file, for example, might contain the item's part number, description, and quantity on hand.

item value   The information assigned to an item.

K   A unit of measure of computer capacity. 1K equals 1024 bytes.

key   The item in a record of a PFS file that is used by the program to find the entire record.

load   To transfer a program from a floppy disk or hard disk to the computer memory.

log on   To initiate use of an information utility, PAMS, or communication service by entering an account number and password.

"LPT1:"   The name of the first parallel device driver in the IBM PC or XT.

"LPT2:"   The name of the second parallel device driver in the IBM PC or XT.

Main Menu   The first menu that is displayed when a PFS program is started.

menu   A list of functions or options from which you can choose in order to initiate a procedure.

merge   The transfer of files from different diskettes to form one file.

modem   A device that enables computers to communicate over telephone lines; it converts computer signals to a form that can be sent over a telephone line and converts telephone line signals to a form that can be interpreted by a computer.

operating system   A program that manages or supervises the computer's operation, its execution of programs, and manipulation of data. It allows the user to enter commands to the computer, manage files, and control input and output operations (see also DOS).

option   A selection from any menu, except the Main Menu, that initiates an operation.

PAMS   A *public access message system*: a system left online for access by virtually any computer user. Often no account number or password is necessary for access. Also called BBS (bulletin board system) or CBBS (computerized bulletin board system).

parallel port   A computer channel in which the information is transmitted to printers or external devices as an entire character, that is, eight bits at a time. This is the most common type of interface used by the IBM PC and XT for printers. It is not used for modems (see serial port).

parity   A bit used (optionally) in the transmission of each character to ensure accurate transmission. Parity bits are used in information transfers using the COM1: and COM2: ports (see COM1: and COM2:).

PC DOS   See DOS.

prompt   A symbol or message—such as "A>" in DOS—that indicates the computer's readiness to receive a command or information.

record   A single entity in a file of information. A record is made up of one or more items in a form used by a PFS file. For example, the collection of information (that is, items) identifying one part in an inventory file or one mailing address would make up one record. In the PFS manuals, both forms and records are called forms.

retrieval   The process of searching for information on a disk to display it on the screen.

retrieval specifications   The information that identifies to the program what is to be retrieved.

root directory   See directory.

RS-232C   A standard for the connectors and cable used to connect a modem or a serial printer to a computer.

serial port   A computer channel in which the information is transmitted to printers, modems, or other external devices a byte at a time (see parallel port). The serial interface is the most common type of interface for stand-alone modems.

stop bit   In a serial transmission, the bit used to indicate the end of each character.

wild-card character   A character used to represent any other character or group of characters. In PFS:WRITE, the asterisk is used as a wild-card character in a search.

wordwrap   An action in which the computer automatically moves a word to the next line if there is not room on the current line.

write-protect tab   A piece of tape placed over the notch in the jacket of a diskette to prevent the computer from writing to the disk or erasing anything on it.

APPENDIX
B

PFS Hardware Requirements

For proper operation, PFS products require certain hardware configurations.

COMPUTERS

The PFS products will run on the IBM PC and PC-compatible computers from other manufacturers. The few products that will not run on certain machines are identified in parentheses.

IBM PC and IBM XT
IBM PCjr (PFS:GRAPH is not available)
Corona
Eagle
Compaq and Compaq Plus
Hyperion (PFS:GRAPH will not run)
Columbia Data Products MPC
Chameleon (PFS:FILE and PFS:REPORT only)
Mindset

218

Special versions of some PFS products are available for some computers that are not PC-compatible:

TI Professional: PFS:FILE, PFS:REPORT, PFS:GRAPH
Apple II: PFS:FILE, PFS:REPORT, PFS:GRAPH
Apple IIc and IIe: all PFS products
Apple III: PFS:FILE, PFS:REPORT, PFS:GRAPH
Apple Macintosh: PFS:FILE, PFS:REPORT

Before purchasing a PFS product, check with your dealer to be sure it will operate on your specific computer.

PFS MEMORY REQUIREMENTS

All PFS programs described in this book require 128K of memory or more.

PERIPHERALS REQUIRED

Most PFS programs have similar peripheral requirements, but there are some differences.

PFS:WRITE Requirements

You need an 80-column video monitor with a monochrome adapter or a color/graphics adapter card. You will also need one of the following printers: IBM Graphics, Epson, Okidata, IDS, NEC, or C. Itoh.

PFS:FILE Requirements

You need an 80-column video monitor. A monochrome display will be easier to read. You will also need a serial or parallel printer. Almost any type of printer will work. Two disk drives are recommended.

NOTE: Each page of a form is stored as one or more 128-byte blocks. A blank page will also be stored as a block.

PFS:REPORT Requirements

You will need an 80-character video monitor. A monochrome monitor is suggested to improve contrast. A serial or parallel printer is also required, and can be of almost any type.

PFS:GRAPH Requirements

You will need a monitor capable of displaying graphics. With an IBM PC you will need a color/graphics adapter card. Some systems, such as the COMPAQ, have built-in graphics capability.

You will also need *either* or *both* of the following:

- A serial or parallel printer that is one of the following types: IBM Graphics Printer, IBM 80 CPS Matrix Printer with graphics option; Epson MX-70, MX-80, MX-100, or FX-80; Okidata 82, 83, 92, or 93; IDS Prism without color option; NEC 8023; or C. Itoh ProWriter.

- One of the following plotters: HP 7470, HIPLOT DMP-29 or DMP-40, Strobe 100, or Sweet-P.

Note that if you use an IBM PC, you will need a Color/Graphics Color Adapter card and preferably a color monitor. For high-quality graphs, you will need a plotter. Many of the better dot matrix printers (such as the Okidata 93) do an excellent job of printing graphs.

PFS:ACCESS Requirements

You will need one of the following modems:

Bizcomp PC Intellimodem
Hayes SmartModem 300, 1200, or 1200B
IBM PCjr built-in
Novation 103 or 212 Smart-Cat
Prentice POPCOM X100
US Robotics Password
Transcend PC Modem Card 300 or 1200
Ven-Tel PC Modem Plus

You will also need a video monitor. A monochrome display will be easier to read. A color monitor can be used. A serial or parallel printer is optional but suggested.

Suggested printers include the IBM color printer or graphics printer, C. Itoh, Epson, Okidata, IDS, or NEC printers.

APPENDIX
C

Installing
PFS Products

Before you can use a PFS program, it must be *installed* for your particular system — your computer, your monitor, and your peripherals such as your printer. *Installation* is the setting up of the program to run on your particular hardware. Normally the program must be installed before it can be used, and installation does not need to be done again unless you are making changes in your system — say, because you have bought a new printer.

THE OPERATING SYSTEM
AND PFS PRODUCTS

The operating system is a collection of programs that act like the manager or supervisor of your computer. When you boot, or start, the computer, the operating system is automatically loaded to the computer. In response to the user's commands, the operating system selects the program to be executed and provides a number of support functions, such as formatting and copying disks, listing the directory, and listing files.

The IBM PC, PC XT, and PCjr use the PC DOS operating system. PC DOS is available in several versions: 1.0, 1.1, 2.0, and 2.1. However, for convenience DOS 1.0 and 1.1 are referred to in this book as DOS 1, and DOS 2.0 and 2.1 are called DOS 2. PFS products designed for the IBM PC can be used with any version of PC DOS and with many of the IBM-compatible computers using MS DOS (see Appendix B).

To install any PFS product on your computer, you will need to complete one or more of five procedures:

1. Create a backup copy.

2. Install the operating system on the program disk.

3. Set up the program for your specific printer.

4. Set the default drive.

5. Create a routine to initialize the printer when the program is started.

How many procedures you must use and which ones they are will depend upon the PFS product and your system. However, you will never use all five procedures with any one product, so it is important to know which of these to use and in what order.

If you have a hard disk, you will also want to install your PFS products on it.

This appendix guides you through the procedures for installing PFS:WRITE and then shows you how to vary these procedures to install the other PFS programs described in this book.

INSTALLING PFS:WRITE

Your first step is to decide whether your operating system — PC DOS or MS DOS — will fit on the PFS:WRITE program disk. If you are using a floppy disk system, PC DOS 1 will fit and PC DOS 2 will not fit. If you are using a version of MS DOS, check with your dealer to see if there is room on the disk. If there is room, follow the procedure for installing DOS 1; if there is not room, follow the procedure for installing DOS 2. If you are using a hard disk, your first procedure is to install PFS:WRITE on the hard disk.

Installing DOS on the Program Disk

To install DOS, choose the appropriate procedure from the following:

Using an IBM PC with DOS 1 and a single floppy disk drive Place the DOS disk in the drive and turn on your computer system. When prompted, enter the correct date and time. When the DOS prompt, "A>", appears, remove the DOS disk. Be sure there is *no* write-protect tab on the PFS:WRITE disk or covering of any kind over the notch on the disk. If the notch is covered, the computer will not be able to write the operating system to the disk. Place the PFS:WRITE program disk in the drive. Enter

A>**INSTALL** ENTER

The install program will load and the following message will be displayed:

PAUSE place DOS diskette in drive B,
leave PFS series diskette in drive A
Strike any key when ready...

Ignore the message to change disks and press any key. The following message will then be displayed

Insert diskette for drive B and strike any key when ready

You have no Drive B, so remove the PFS:WRITE disk, put the DOS disk in the drive, and press any key. Soon the following message will be displayed:

Insert diskette for drive A and strike any key when ready

Remove the DOS disk and again place the PFS:WRITE disk in the drive. Press any key. Continue in this way, inserting the PFS:WRITE program disk when the computer asks for a disk insertion in Drive A and inserting the DOS system disk when the computer asks for a disk insertion in Drive B. When the DOS prompt, "A>", appears, the installation of the operating system is completed and you can begin using PFS:WRITE. The program disk can now be inserted in Drive A to boot the system.

Do not cover the disk notch with a write-protect tab yet, because you still need to follow the procedure to install the program for your specific printer and monitor.

Using an IBM PC with DOS 2 and a single floppy disk drive   DOS 2 cannot be installed on the PFS:WRITE program disk because there is insufficient space. Go to the next section, "Installing for Monitor and Printer."

Using an IBM PC with DOS 1 and dual floppy disk drives   Place the DOS disk in Drive A and turn on your computer system. Enter the correct date and time when prompted. When the DOS prompt, "A>", appears, remove the DOS disk, put it in Drive B, and place the PFS:WRITE program disk in Drive A. Be sure there is *no* write-protect tab on the PFS:WRITE disk. Enter

   A>**INSTALL** ENTER

The INSTALL program will load. The following message will then be displayed:

   PAUSE place DOS diskette in drive B,
   leave PFS series diskette in drive A
   Strike any key when ready...

Since you have already put the DOS disk in Drive B, press any key. You will then see the disk lights flash and the monitor display some messages as the operating system is copied to the disk in Drive A. When the DOS prompt, "A>", appears, the installation of the operating system is completed and you can begin using PFS:WRITE. The program disk can now be inserted in Drive A to boot the computer. Do not cover the disk notch with a write-protect tab yet, because you may need to install the PFS:WRITE program for your printer and monitor, as described in the next section.

Using an IBM PC with DOS 2 and dual floppy disk drives   DOS 2 cannot be installed on the PFS:WRITE program disk; there is not enough space. Go to the next section, "Installing for Monitor and Printer."

Using an IBM XT or hard disk system   The PFS:WRITE program can be installed on the hard disk and used directly from the hard disk. The hard disk must have at least two megabytes of storage available. The program can be installed on the main (or root) directory or a sub-directory, but all files referenced by PFS:WRITE must be on the same directory. You cannot use the DOS COPY program to install the program on the hard disk. You must use a special utility called

HARDDISK, which is on the sampler disk that came with your program. Turn your computer on and enter the date and time when the system requests these. Wait until you see the system prompt, "C>". Place the PFS:WRITE *sampler* disk in Drive A, log to this drive, and enter the name of the utility program as

C>A: ENTER
A>**HARDDISK** ENTER

The program will ask for identification of the drive in which you have placed the sampler disk. Since Drive A is identified by default, press F10 to continue. The program will then ask for the target disk drive or the designator for the hard disk drive on which you will install PFS:WRITE. If you have an IBM PC XT with the hard disk configured as Drive C, enter **C** and press F10. If your floppy disk drive is not A and the hard disk is not C, you should enter the appropriate drive designators when using HARDDISK.

When this copy operation is completed, remove the sampler diskette and place the PFS:WRITE program disk in Drive A. Be sure there is no write-protect tab on the program disk. Press F10 again, and the PFS:WRITE program will be copied to the hard disk. This will take a while. After the copy operation is completed, you will see the message

COPY COMPLETED

Remove the PFS:WRITE program disk and store it in a safe place. The program can only be installed to the hard disk from the program diskette five times. Since you get one spare program disk with PFS:WRITE, this means you can install the program a total of ten times.

Installing for Monitor and Printer

Your second procedure is to install the program for your specific monitor and printer. The PFS:WRITE program comes installed for the IBM monochrome display, a monochrome display adapter, and almost any type of parallel printer connected to DOS device "LPT1:". If your system fits this description, your installation is complete: you can put a write-protect tab on your program disk and begin using your PFS:WRITE program. If you are using any other type of monitor or a serial printer, you must modify your program by following the steps described next. These steps make use of the SETWRITE utility program that is on your sampler disk.

If you are using a floppy disk system, put the PFS:WRITE *sampler* disk in Drive A. This disk contains the SETWRITE program you will need. If you are using a hard disk, SETWRITE was copied to the hard disk when you installed PFS:WRITE to it. To be sure this program is now on your hard disk, use the DOS command "DIR" so you can check your directory. You can then log to the hard disk and continue.

In response to the system prompt, enter the following:

A>**SETWRITE** ENTER

NOTE: If you are using a hard disk, be sure the prompt is for Drive C ("C>") instead of A.

After the program loads, you will see the screen shown in Figure C-1. If at any time you wish to abort the setup—that is, to bring the procedure to a halt without changing your program—you can press ESC. If

```
                    PFS:WRITE SET UP
                    ---------------


        This program sets up your computer's display system for use

        by PFS:WRITE, provides PFS:WRITE with the correct DOS

        device name for your printer, and sets up the Asynchronous

        Communications Adaptor for a serial printer.


            Place your PFS:WRITE program diskette in drive A.

        If you make a mistake, press ESC and run this program again.

            (C) 1983 Software Publishing Corporation

                                          F10-Continue
```

Figure C-1. *Starting the PFS:WRITE setup*

you do so, you must enter **SETWRITE** again to resume the setup procedure. To continue the setup, put your program disk in Drive A and press F10. You will now see the Default Setup Menu (Figure C-2). On the menu are two options. For the first option, "USING COLOR MONITOR", enter **N** (for "no") unless you have a color monitor. If you have a monochrome monitor, a color adapter card without a color monitor, or a Compaq computer, you must enter **N**. Enter **Y** only if you are using a color monitor.

```
                    DEFAULT SETUP MENU
                    ------------------




              USING COLOR MONITOR (Y/N): N

              DEFAULT PRINT TO: LPT1:






                                         F10-Continue
```

Figure C-2.   PFS:WRITE Default Setup Menu

The second prompt, "DEFAULT PRINT TO:", can be used to change the DOS printer device. It will default to "LPT1", the normal printer driver for systems with a parallel printer. If you are using a different DOS device, enter the correct device. Parallel printers should be "LPT1:", "LPT2:", or "LPT3:". Serial printers should be "COM1:" or "COM2:". If necessary, change to the correct device (TAB to the "DEFAULT PRINT TO:" option if necessary) and press F10. If you select a COM1: or COM2: device, a COM Setup Menu will be displayed. (Figure C-3 shows the COM1 Setup Menu.) Enter the correct baud rate, parity, byte length, and the number of stop bits to this menu and press F10 again. These values must be correct for your specific computer system. You can obtain them from your dealer.

```
COM1 SETUP MENU




BAUD RATE: 1200

PARITY (NONE,ODD,EVEN): NONE

BYTE LENGTH (7 OR 8): 8

NUMBER OF STOP BITS (1 OR 2): 1
```

Figure C-3.   *Setting up a serial printer*

Your program is now installed. If you are using a floppy disk system, place a write-protect tab on your program disk before continuing.

INSTALLING PFS:FILE

The PFS:FILE program occupies less disk space than the PFS:WRITE program, so if you are using a floppy disk system you can install your operating system, whether it is DOS 1 or DOS 2, on the program disk. This installation should be your first step. Follow the procedures described in the previous section for installing DOS 1 on the PFS:WRITE program disk. Those procedures are correct for any MS DOS or PC DOS system using PFS:FILE.

Your second procedure is to install PFS:FILE for your printer and select the drive for your work disk. The procedure is very similar to the printer installation described in the previous section on PFS:WRITE, but with two differences: first, the installation program is called SETUP. Second, SETUP is on the program disk, not on a separate sampler disk. To install your printer, put the program disk in Drive A and enter the name of the program:

A>**SETUP** ENTER

You will see an Option Select screen that is very similar to the **PFS:WRITE SETUP** screen except that it invites you to select a work drive. If you are using a floppy disk system with two drives, enter **B**. (If you have a single-drive system, you will not be able to do any of the operations, such as sorting, that require a second drive for a work drive.) Press F10 when you have completed your option entry.

If you are using a hard disk system, the installation of **PFS:FILE** also resembles that of **PFS:WRITE** with the changes just described. *But there is one additional critical difference:* The SETUP program must be installed *before* you install the program to the hard disk. It is very important that you follow the correct sequence. You can install the **PFS:FILE** program to the hard disk only five times, and if you forget to call SETUP before installing the **PFS:FILE** program to the hard disk, the installation will fail but will nevertheless be counted as one of the five. You will have to start over again, installing the program to the hard disk a second time after you install SETUP. The **PFS:FILE** program is then installed to the hard disk with the HARDDISK program, as described in the previous section on **PFS:WRITE**. The only difference is that the HARDDISK program is on the program disk and not the sampler disk, so the installation is started with the program disk in the floppy disk drive.

There may be times when you wish to send special codes to your printer whenever the printer is turned on. For example, you might want to set the printer to a compressed mode when wide reports are to be printed on standard 8 1/2 × 11-inch paper. You could use a simple BASIC program, or you could use a third installation procedure, whether your system is floppy disk or hard disk. You use the PRINTER utility program that is on the disk with **PFS:FILE**. This utility can be copied to the hard disk or run from the floppy disk. Start the program with

A>**PRINTER** ENTER

You will then see the Printer Setup screen (Figure C-4). Leave the DOS device as displayed ("LPT1:"), or change it to another device if necessary. Press F10. You will then see the work screen shown in Figure C-5. Enter whatever characters you wish to send to the printer and press F10 when you have finished. The codes will be sent to the printer immediately.

With some printers you will need to repeat this operation whenever the printer is turned on. With other printers, the settings will be remembered even if the printer has been turned off. Experiment with your printer to see what is necessary.

```
                    PRINTER SETUP


       This program allows you to send special characters to a printer.
          Turn your printer off and on, and enter its name below.



                      PRINTER NAME: LPT1:



            (C) 1982 Software Publishing Corporation
                                                    F10-Continue
```

Figure C-4.   *The printer setup*

```
          Enter printer setup characters.  Press F10 when done.
                 The characters will be sent to the printer.
       If you make a mistake, press F6 to escape from the program,
                     and then run the program again.
```

Figure C-5.   *Instructions to enter the printer codes*

Another alternative is to set the codes up as a small BASIC program and call the program using a batch file. For example, with an Okidata 93 printer the following BASIC program sets the printer to compressed print:

```
5 REM DRAFT17 PROGRAM
10 LPRINT CHR$(27);CHR$(48)
15 LPRINT CHR$(29)
20 SYSTEM
```

This program can be saved as "DRAFT17.BAS" and can be called from a batch file that has only a single line:

BASICA DRAFT17

The batch file is called "DRAFT17.BAT." To start the compressed print, you would need to enter only:

A>**DRAFT17** ENTER

INSTALLING PFS:REPORT

PFS:REPORT is installed on a floppy disk or hard disk system exactly as PFS:FILE is installed. On a floppy disk system you

1. Copy the operating system to the disk
2. Run SETUP to install the program for your printer
3. Use PRINTER, if necessary, to define any starting printer codes.

On a hard disk system, you run SETUP first and then install the PFS:REPORT program to the hard disk with HARDDISK.

INSTALLING PFS:GRAPH

To install PFS:GRAPH, you must have a color/graphics adapter and a color monitor. Otherwise the program cannot be installed for your printer. If you are using an IBM-compatible computer, check with your dealer before starting to be sure you have all the hardware necessary to support PFS:GRAPH.

If you are using a floppy disk system, DOS 2 cannot be installed on the program disk, but DOS 1 can. If you have the latter, follow the DOS installation procedure given for PFS:WRITE. If you have a hard disk, also follow the procedures given in that section.

The second procedure is to install PFS:GRAPH for your printer. PFS:GRAPH can be used with a printer or plotter or both. The PFS:GRAPH program comes installed for an IBM Graphics Printer and an HP plotter. If you have these, you can put a write-protect tab on your program disk and skip this section. If you are using any other type of printer, you must modify your program by following the steps now described.

If you are using a two-drive floppy disk system, put the **PFS:GRAPH** *sampler* disk in Drive A. This contains the SETGRAPH program you will need. If you are using a hard disk, it is suggested that *before* you install PFS:GRAPH on the disk you first run SETGRAPH and install the program for your printer and plotter. You can then install the PFS:GRAPH program on your hard disk.

When you have the DOS prompt, "A>", put the **PFS:GRAPH** program in Drive A if it is not already there, and enter the following in response:

A>**SETGRAPH** ENTER

After the program loads, you will see the SETUP message screen. If at any time you wish to abort the setup without changing your program, press ESC. To continue the setup, do *not* press F10; instead press PGDN. You will then see the Default Printer screen. Locate your printer in the list on the screen and enter the number given there for your printer. Enter the DOS device number. The DOS device defaults to "LPT1:".

Press PGDN to continue to the next screen, the Default Plotter Selection screen. This screen defaults to the HP plotter on DOS device COM1:. If necessary, enter the number for a different plotter or DOS device. If you are not using a plotter, leave the default values as displayed. If any of the previous screens did not select a COM device (you are using a parallel port), you can press F10 and the setup is completed. If you selected one or more serial ports, press PGDN again. This will give a screen that enables you to set the values for the serial port (speed, parity, stop bits, byte length). If you selected only one serial port, you can press F10. If you have to set another serial port, press PGDN again and set this screen. Either PGDN or F10 will complete the setup at this point.

INSTALLING PFS:ACCESS

Unlike other PFS products, the **PFS:ACCESS** program disk does not come with a spare copy. However, you can create *one* copy of the disk. You should do so before doing anything else—even if you plan to use

PFS:ACCESS with a hard disk. To create the backup, you will need one blank double-sided, double-density disk. It does not need to be formatted before using. You should then follow the procedure that suits your system:

IBM PC or XT with one floppy disk drive and DOS 1 or DOS 2

Start DOS and log to Drive A. Insert the PFS:ACCESS program disk into Drive A and enter

A>**BACKUP** ENTER

You will then see the screen in Figure C-6. Remove the program disk and put the blank disk in the drive. Press ENTER. The blank disk will be formatted. Upon request, put the program disk back in the drive and press ENTER again. At the next prompt, replace the disk with your blank disk again. Continue to swap the disks, following the prompts to be sure you are putting the right disk in each time. When the copy is completed, the DOS prompt, "A>", will appear again and you will see a message confirming that the copy has been completed normally. Remove your new backup disk and label it with a felt pen. Store the original disk in a safe place and use the backup.

```
A) backup
PFS Software Series
program backup utility

(C) 1984 Software Publishing Corp.

Have your PFS program
diskette and a blank
double-density, double-sided
diskette ready.

Place the PFS program
diskette in drive A: and the
blank diskette in drive B:
and press Enter when ready.


Note: If you are not ready for this
operation, press Esc.
```

Figure C-6. Starting the backup

IBM PC or XT with two floppy disk drives and DOS 1 or DOS 2

Start DOS and log to Drive A. Insert the PFS:ACCESS program disk in Drive A and enter

A>**BACKUP** ENTER

You will then see the screen in Figure C-6. Place your blank disk in Drive B and press ENTER. The blank disk will be formatted and the program copied to it all in one process. Next you will see a message that the backup is completed normally and the DOS prompt will be displayed. Remove your new program disk, label it with a felt pen, and store the original in a safe place. Use your new disk as your program disk.

Your next procedure is to configure your program for your particular printer and monitor. The program, as delivered, is set to work with an IBM monochrome display and a parallel printer. If you have a serial printer or are using the Color/Graphics Adapter, you will need to run the SETUP program to configure the printer for your system. To do so, place your PFS:ACCESS disk in Drive A, boot the system, and enter the date if necessary to get the DOS prompt. Enter the name of the setup program:

A>**SETUP** ENTER

You will then see the screen of Figure C-7. Read the screen and press ENTER. You will then see the Setup Menu of Figure C-8. If you need to change the printer, select function 1 (Select a Printer) from this menu and press ENTER. You will then see the Printer Selection Menu (Figure C-9). Enter the number that corresponds to your printer. You will then be asked the DOS device name. This is normally "LPT1:". If this is different on your system, enter the correct device. Next press ENTER. If you select a serial printer, you will see the serial setup screen and must enter the information for the serial port (speed, byte length, stop bits, and parity). After the setup is complete, you will see the message

PFS:ACCESS - OK

After the printer installation is complete, you are returned to the Setup Menu. If you need to set up the system for a color monitor, select function 2 (Turn Color Off or On) and answer the single question with a **Y**. If you do not need to install the program on the hard disk, the

```
A)setup

PFS: Software Series SETUP Program
Copr. 1984 Software Publishing Corp.

This is the SETUP utility for the
following PFS: programs:

   PFS:ACCESS

SETUP modifies these programs to work
with different equipment, such as a
serial printer or a fixed disk.

Choose any option from the SETUP menu,
and answer the questions that appear.
If you make a mistake, press Escape to
return to the SETUP menu and try
again.

Press Enter to continue
```

Figure C-7.   *Starting the PFS:ACCESS setup*

```
SETUP Main menu

1.   Select a printer
2.   Turn color off or on
3.   Install program on fixed disk
4.   Exit to DOS

Selection:
```

Figure C-8.   *Setup Main Menu*

installation is now complete and you can select function 4 (Exit to DOS).

If you have an IBM PC XT or another computer with a hard disk, you will want to install PFS:ACCESS on your hard disk. You will need at least two megabytes of free space on the hard disk. You can install the program on the hard disk only five times from each program disk. Since

```
Select Printer

1.   IBM Color Printer
2.   IBM Graphics Printer
3.   C. Itoh
4.   Epson
5.   Epson with Graftrax Plus
6.   IDS
7.   NEC
8.   Okidata
9.   Other

Selection:
```

Figure C-9.   *Selecting the printer*

you have two copies (one original and the copy you made), this gives you the capability of ten installations.

To start the disk installation, remove the write-protect tab from the program disk. Bring up the Setup Menu as you did in installing your printer. From the Setup Menu select function 3 (Install Program on Fixed Disk). You will then need to enter the name of the disk drive designator for the hard disk. This is usually "C" for the IBM PC XT with a single hard disk drive. Enter the appropriate designator followed by a colon. Press ENTER to continue and the program will be copied to the hard disk. When completed, you will see the Setup Menu again. Select function 4 (Exit to DOS) to exit the setup program.

APPENDIX
D

Peripherals
For Telecommunicating
With PFS

After you have installed PFS:ACCESS you will need to set up your modem, computer, and PFS:ACCESS to work together. This appendix tells you how this is done.

WHAT YOU NEED

In order to begin using your IBM PC for electronic communications, you will need the following items:

- PFS:ACCESS program.
- A black and white or color monitor.
- A telephone with a standard jack.
- A modem that can be used with the PFS:ACCESS serial card if your modem requires it.
- Connecting cables.
- An account number and password for each service you plan to use.

A *modem* is an electronic device that converts the digital information from a computer into analog signals that can travel through telephone lines. Another conversion takes place at the receiving computer. There are a wide variety of modems available, but only selected modems will work with PFS:ACCESS.

Some modems are built-in. To use one, you must open your IBM PC and put the modem card in one of the free slots. The cord that normally plugs into the telephone set is disconnected and plugged into the modem card providing a direct connection between the computer and the telephone lines. Many of the built-in modems also have a second telephone plug on the card, so both the telephone set and the telephone line are connected to the computer. This allows you to use the telephone for normal voice communications without having to disconnect the modem from the telephone line.

If the modem is not built-in, it is called a stand-alone modem. To use this type of modem with your computer and PFS:ACCESS, you will need an asynchronous communications adapter card (also called a serial port card). The IBM XT has this card already built-in. If you have an IBM PC, you will have to purchase this card. You will also need a cable to connect the card to the modem. The stand-alone modem is more difficult to connect and use than a built-in modem, but offers more flexibility in case you change your computer later or need to use the modem with more than one system. The stand-alone modem is also more expensive. Like the built-in modem, it connects directly to a standard telephone jack with a standard telephone cord.

Both built-in and stand-alone modems can be purchased for either of two speeds — 300 baud or 1200 baud. If you plan to do a lot of electronic communication, 1200 baud is well worth the additional cost since it is four times faster than 300 baud. Modems have a wide variety of features and vary in cost.

There is one other type of modem that can be used with PFS:ACCESS that should be mentioned. This is the acoustic-coupled modem. Like the stand-alone modem, it requires a serial card and a connecting cable to the computer. Unlike the stand-alone modem, however, it does not connect directly to the telephone line. The acoustic-coupled modem contains two cups, and the telephone handset is placed directly into these cups. It can only be used with a standard handset (no uniquely designed type can be used) and can only be used at 300 baud with most systems. The acoustic modem is inexpensive, but generally lacks features than can be important to a serious user of electronic communications.

To begin electronic communications, you will also need an account number, password, and the telephone numbers of the services you plan to use. These could be public access message systems (PAMS) or information utilities (such as CompuServe or The Source). These are discussed in Chapter 7.

USING A BUILT-IN MODEM

The following built-in modems have been successfully used with PFS:ACCESS:

Bizcomp PC:Intellimodem
Hayes SmartModem 1200B
IBM PCjr built-in
Transcend PC Modem Card or PC Modem Card 1200
Ven-Tel PC Modem Plus or PC Modem Plus 1200.

Before installing your card as a part of your computer, you should examine the card for switches. The following cards have switches that must be set as described:

Hayes Smartmodem 1200B:
  Switch 1: ON with COM1:
       OFF with COM2:

  Switch 2: OFF with a single-line RJ11 jack
       ON with a multi-line RJ12 or RJ13 jack

  Switch 3: ON

Transcend Modems:
  Switch 2: OPEN with COM1:
       CLOSED with COM2:

  All other switches OPEN

Ven-Tel Modems
  Switch 7: UP with a single-line RJ11 jack
       DOWN with a multi-line
       RJ12 or RJ13 jack

  All other switches should be UP

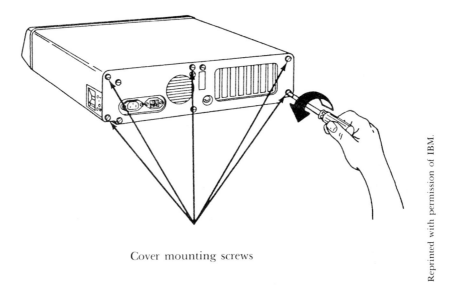

Cover mounting screws

Figure D-1. *Starting to install a built-in modem*

You will need to install this modem inside your IBM PC or XT. Turn the power to your computer and all peripherals off. Examine how the cables at the back of your computer are connected (write this on a piece of paper) and disconnect all the cables. Move the keyboard and monitor away from your work area and be sure you have plenty of work space. Remove the five cover screws from the rear of the system unit (see Figure D-1) and slide the unit's cover forward away from the rear, toward the front (see Figure D-2) and up. Locate an unused slot in the rear of the unit, and use a screwdriver to remove the screw that holds the cover in place for one of the free expansion slots. Save the screw and remove the cover. Place your modem card in the slot and replace the screw. Replace the cover and cover screws carefully. Replace all cables and test your computer to be sure it is functional.

Finally, locate the cable that connects your telephone to the wall jack. Unplug this cable from the telephone set and plug the free end into the proper plug of the built-in modem on the back of your computer. If you

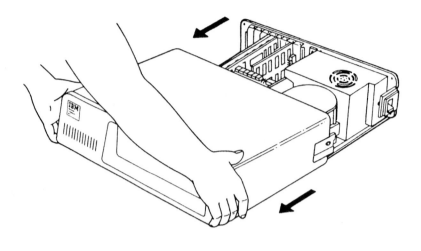

Reprinted with permission of IBM.

Figure D-2. *Opening the IBM cabinet*

have a second plug for the telephone set on the modem card, you may
wish to run another cord from an unused telephone set to the modem
card. Your system should now be ready to use.

USING A STAND-ALONE MODEM

The following stand-alone modems have been successfully used with
PFS:ACCESS:

    Hayes SmartModem 300 or 1200
    Novation 103 Smart-Cat or 103/212 Smart-Cat
    POPCOM X100
    US Robotics Password.

    Set the modem switches in your modem as follows.

Hayes SmartModem 300 or 1200
  Switch 1: UP

  Switch 6: UP

  Switch 7: UP with a single-line RJ11 jack
            DOWN with a multi-line RJ12 or RJ13 jack

  Switch 8: UP

  Other switches can be set to any position.

Novation 103 Smart-Cat or 103/212 Smart-Cat
  If your modem has five switches:

  Switch 3: ON for 300 baud
            OFF for 110 baud

  Switches 1 and 5 should be ON

  Switches 2 and 4 can be in either position.

  If your modem has six switches:
  Switch 4: ON for 300 baud
            OFF for 110 baud

  Switches 2 and 6 should be ON

  Switch 1 should be OFF

  Switches 3 and 5 can be in either position.

NOTE: ON is UP or OPEN
          OFF is DOWN or CLOSED

You will also need an asynchronous communications adapter card. If you have an IBM PC and do not have this card installed, you will need to purchase it. Follow the directions in the last section to open your PC and install the card. Set the switches on the card to use the COM1: port if you are not using a serial printer. If you are using a serial printer, the new serial card will need to be set to the unused serial channel (COM1: or COM2:). If you have an IBM XT, there is already a serial card available that can be used if it is not being used for a printer or other peripheral.

You will also need a cable to connect the asynchronous communications card to the modem. The one you need is called an RS-232C cable; it can be purchased at most stores that sell modems. The wiring for the RS-232C plug on most modems is a standard plug; although all of the asynchronous communications cards use the same RS-232C connection, it could be a connector with pins (as on the IBM XT) or a connector with a socket. There are also two different methods of wiring the connector on the card, and all manufacturers are not consistent. For some products, a normal modem cable can be used. For other serial card products, you will need what is called a *null modem cable*. Whoever sells you the serial card should be able to tell you the type of modem cable you will need for the card. The card determines what type of cable you will need.

Finally, you will need to connect your modem to the telephone line. Locate the cable that connects your telephone to the wall jack. Unplug this cable from the telephone set and plug the free end into the proper plug on the back of the computer that is a part of your modem. If you have a second plug for the telephone set on the card, you may wish to run another cord from the telephone set to the modem card. Your system should now be ready to use.

APPENDIX
E

PFS Command Tables

This appendix summarizes the functions performed by specific keys in each PFS program. You will find that many of the keys perform exactly the same function in each program.

Key	Write	File	Report	Graph	Access
F1	Brings up help menu				Brings up help menu
F2	Sets TABS	Prints all pages of form			Sends output to printer
F3	Moves cursor to previous word	Removes record	Removes report specification		Disconnects from service
CTRL-F3	Moves cursor to beginning of line				
F4	Moves cursor to next word				Stops and saves auto log-on

Key	Write	File	Report	Graph	Access
CTRL-F4	Moves cursor to end of line				
F5	Labels block	Enters current date			Sends a file
CTRL-F5	Erases a word				
F6	Duplicates a block	Enters current time			Saves a file
CTRL-F6	Erases a line				
F7	Initiates a search		Sets up a derived columns screen		
CTRL-F7	Sets up an underline				
F8	Formats a line				
CTRL-F8	Sets up for boldface print				
F9	Appends text				
F10	Continues	Continues or saves current record and continues	Continues	Continues	Continues
ESC	Cancels operation	Cancels operation	Cancels operation	Cancels operation	Cancels operation
TAB	Moves cursor between menu options	Moves cursor between menu options	Moves cursor between menu options	Moves cursor between menu options	Moves cursor between menu options
CTRL-TAB	Moves cursor backward on menu	Moves cursor backward on menu	Moves cursor backward on menu	Moves cursor backward on menu	Moves cursor backward on menu
PGDN	Moves cursor down one screen	Moves cursor down one page	Moves cursor down one page	Moves cursor down one screen	
PGUP	Moves cursor up one screen	Moves cursor up one page	Moves cursor up one page	Moves cursor up one screen	

Key	Write	File	Report	Graph	Access
HOME	Moves cursor to beginning of document	Moves cursor to first item on screen	Moves cursor to first item on screen	Moves cursor to first item on screen	Moves cursor to start of session
CTRL-HOME		Erases current page	Erases current page	Erases current page	
END	Moves cursor to end of document				Returns to transmission line
INS	Inserts a character at cursor location	Inserts a character at cursor location	Inserts a character at cursor location	Inserts a character at cursor location	Inserts a character at cursor location
DEL	Deletes a character at cursor location	Deletes a character at cursor location	Deletes a character at cursor location	Deletes a character at cursor location	Deletes a character at cursor location
BACKSPACE	Moves cursor one space to the left and erases last character	Moves cursor one space to the left and erases last character	Moves cursor one space to the left and erases last character	Moves cursor one space to the left and erases last character	Moves cursor one space to the left and erases last character
CURSOR CONTROL	Moves cursor one space in the direction of the arrow	Moves cursor one space in the direction of the arrow	Moves cursor one space in the direction of the arrow	Moves cursor one space in the direction of the arrow	Moves cursor one space in the direction of the arrow

APPENDIX
F

File-Naming Conventions

When using your PFS products, you should devise a standard procedure for naming files and using disks. Chapter 6 described how to use PFS:FILE and PFS:REPORT to manage your disk library. In this appendix you will learn the conventions for assigning extensions to your file names.

Certain file name extensions have reserved meanings for PC DOS and MS DOS and should not be used for your files. The following are some extensions you should avoid and their applications:

ASM   Assembly source programs

BAS   BASIC source code

BAT   Batch processing files

BLD   BASIC BLOAD format

CAL   Spreadsheet files

COB   COBOL source files

COM   Executable programs

EXE   Executable programs, relocation format

FOR   FORTRAN source programs

LIB   Library routines

OBJ   Program object code

PAS   Pascal source files

$$$ Temporary files

In the examples in this book, the following extensions are used in naming files:

Program	Extension	File Type	Input/Output
PFS:WRITE	LTR	Letters	I/O
	DOC	Documents	I/O
	BAK	Backups (all)	I/O
PFS:FILE	DAT	Data Files	I/O
	BAK	Backups	I/O
	PRN	ASCII File Image	O
PFS:REPORT	DAT	Data Files	I
	PRN	Report Image	O
PFS:GRAPH	DAT	Data Files	I
	DIF	Spreadsheet Data	I
	CHT	Chart Data	I/O
	PIC	Graph Image	O
PFS:ACCESS	PRN	ASCII Data Files	I/O
	DOC	Document Files	I/O

At any time you can change any of these extensions except PIC. It is advisable, however, to define extension names at the beginning that relate to your environment and to use these consistently in your work.

APPENDIX
G

Using PFS Products
With Other Computers

The main text of this book has been written specifically for IBM PC and IBM PC XT users. However, PFS software is also available for the Apple IIe, IIc, and III, as well as the TI Professional. This appendix outlines how the PFS programs work on these computers to enable Apple and TI owners to use this book.

USING PFS PRODUCTS
WITH THE APPLE IIe AND IIc

The following discussion analyzes each of the PFS products applicable to the Apple IIe and IIc.

PFS:WRITE

Hardware requirements are the Apple IIe with 64K of memory, an 80-column monitor, a printer, and a single disk drive. A second disk drive is useful but optional.

The Get function on the PFS:WRITE Main Menu can only be used to retrieve PFS:WRITE documents. The JOIN command functions correctly to join reports or PFS:WRITE documents as well as reports created with the APPLE IIe/IIc PFS:REPORT.

The CTRL-C combination is used instead of F10 to continue a function. The following control codes are used:

CTRL-A	Append a document
CTRL-B	Boldface
CTRL-C	Continue
CTRL-D	Duplicate a block
CTRL-E	Erase a line
CTRL-F	Format (justify) a line
CTRL-GB	Go to the beginning of a document
CTRL-GE	Go to the end of a document
CTRL-L	Label a block
CTRL-N	Next page
CTRL-P	Previous page
CTRL-R	Remove characters or blocks
CTRL-S	Initiate a search
CTRL-T	Set tabs
CTRL-W	Delete word
CTRL-Y	Start insert
CTRL-\	Start underline

The Apple key can also be used with other keys to move the cursor word by word to the beginning or end of a line or to get a help screen.

PFS:FILE

Hardware requirements for PFS:FILE are the same as for PFS:WRITE. Optional equipment includes a second disk drive (if the Copy function is used), an 80-column video card, a printer, and a printer interface card.
  The following maximum specifications apply:

- 80 characters/line, 1679 characters/item, 100 items/page
- 40 characters/line, 839 characters/item, 50 items/page
- 32 pages/form, 1000 forms/file, 1 file/disk
- 2.5 seconds for an average item search
- 162 seconds maximum for a sequential search.

Some printer cards will not work with PFS products. Since the PFS products for all computers are written in Pascal, you can only use cards that will work with Pascal. The following printer cards have been successfully used with PFS:FILE and the Apple IIe or IIc:

- All Apple cards
- Epson parallel and serial
- Tymac serial
- Grappler and Grappler+
- PKASO EP12
- MPI card
- Mountain Computer CPS
- Microbuffer card (2.3)
- CCS 7710A and 7729
- Prometheus Versacard and Graphitti (2.3).

The following printer cards will *not* work, since they are not Pascal-compatible:

- SSM ASIO and SSM APIO
- Axiom card
- CCS 7728.

You cannot print to a file from PFS:FILE as you can with the IBM PC version. You cannot enter data to a file from another program.

The following control codes are effective:

CTRL-C	Continue
CTRL-E	Clear a form
CTRL-N	Next page
CTRL-D	Print all form pages
CTRL-P	Previous page
CTRL-R	Remove all form pages
ESC	Return to menu

PFS:REPORT

The hardware requirements for **PFS:REPORT** are the same as for **PFS:WRITE**. Optional requirements are a second disk drive (if sorting is done), an 80-character card, and a Pascal-compatible printer card and printer (see PFS:FILE).

The following maximum specifications apply:

- 9 columns/sorted report
- 7 columns/unsorted report
- 2 sorted columns/report
- 3 derived columns/report
- 160 characters/report line
- 40 characters sorted/item.

Only data entered from PFS:FILE can be used in reports (see Chapter 5). The following control codes can be used:

CTRL-A	Switch between two 40-column horizontal parts
CTRL-C	Continue
CTRL-D	Display derived columns screen
CTRL-N	Next page
CTRL-P	Previous page
CTRL-R	Remove report specification or heading
ESC	Return to menu

PFS:GRAPH

The hardware requirements for PFS:GRAPH are the same as for PFS:WRITE except that a graphic printer is also needed. The following printers have been successfully used with PFS:GRAPH and the Apple IIe and Apple IIc.

Apple Silenttype
Epson MX-70, MX-80, MX-100, FX-80 with Graphtrax or
   Graphtrax+
Apple Dot Matrix
Okidata 82A or 83A with Okigraph 1
IDS Prism with Dot Plot
NEC 8023
C. Itoh ProWriter

Other printers can be used if they are compatible with one of those listed. One of the Pascal interface cards must also be used. A color monitor and a second disk drive are both optional.

The following maximum specifications apply:

- 36 points/graph

- 4 graphs/chart

- 45 charts/disk

- 8 segments/pie graph

- 15 characters/legend or identifier

- 26 characters/chart title

- 26 characters/axis label.

Color:

    31 bars/graph (numeric or data)
    15 bars/graph (identifier)
    No pie charts in color.

Input data can be from DIF files created by spreadsheet programs such as VisiCalc or from files created with PFS:FILE. Output PIC files can be created (Chapter 6).

USING PFS PRODUCTS WITH THE APPLE III

PFS:FILE, REPORT, and GRAPH are available for the Apple III. There is a slight variation in how the products are used and specified from the IBM PC version.

PFS:FILE

Hardware requirements are the Apple III with 128K of memory, an 80-column monitor, a printer, and a single disk drive. Optional equipment includes a second disk drive (if the Copy function is used) or a ProFile hard disk, a printer, and a printer interface card.

The following maximum specifications apply:

- 1679 characters/item

- 100 items/page

- 32 pages/form

- 1000 forms/floppy disk file

- 32000 forms/hard disk file

- 1 file/disk

- 2.1 seconds for item exact match on floppy disk
- 1.2 seconds for item exact match on hard disk
- 162 seconds maximum for a sequential search on floppy disk
- 105 seconds maximum for a sequential search on a hard disk.

You can write to a file from PFS:FILE just as you can with the IBM PC version. You cannot enter data to a file from another program. A List Files option on the menu shows you what files are in use.

The following control codes are effective:

CTRL-C	Continue
CTRL-E	Clear a form
CTRL-N	Next page
CTRL-O	Print all form pages
CTRL-P	Previous page
CTRL-R	Remove all form pages
ESC	Return to menu

PFS:REPORT

The hardware requirements are the same as for PFS:FILE. Optional requirements include a second disk drive (if sorting is done) or a ProFile hard disk and printer (see PFS:FILE).

The following maximum specifications apply:

- 20 columns/sorted report
- 18 columns/unsorted report, one disk drive
- 2 sorted columns/report
- 3 derived columns/report
- 255 characters/report line
- 40 characters sorted/item.

PFS:REPORT can write to a disk file, and reports can be included in documents created with PFS:WRITE. As with the IBM PC version, you cannot print reports from data created with "foreign" programs. Only data entered from PFS:FILE can be used in reports.

The following control codes can be used:

CTRL-C   Continue

CTRL-D   Display derived columns screen

CTRL-N   Next page

CTRL-P   Previous page

CTRL-R   Remove pre-defined report

CTRL-S   Send control codes to printer

ESC   Return to menu

PFS:GRAPH

The hardware requirements are the same as for PFS:FILE except that a graphics printer is needed. The following printers have been successfully used with PFS:GRAPH and the Apple III:

- Epson MX-70, MX-80, MX-100

- Okidata 82A

- Applie Dot Matrix

- IDS Prism

- NEC 8023

- C. Itoh ProWriter.

Some printers may need a graphics extension. Other printers can be used if they are compatible with one of the listed printers. A Hewlett Packard HP7470A plotter can also be used.

The following maximum specifications apply:

- 36 points/graph

- 4 graphs/chart

- 45 charts/disk
- 8 segments/pie graph
- 15 characters/legend or identifier
- 26 characters/chart title
- 26 characters/axis label.

Color:

31 bars/graph (numeric or data)
15 bars/graph (identifier)
No pie charts in color.

Input data can be from DIF files created by a spreadsheet program such as VisiCalc or from files created with PFS:FILE. Output PIC files can be created.

USING PFS PRODUCTS WITH THE TI PROFESSIONAL

The directions for using the PFS products with the TI Professional Computer are almost identical to those for the IBM PC. The specifications, as well, are almost identical. The only difference is that the TI Professional does not have the PGDN and PGUP keys. To page up, use the ALT key with the up arrow. To page down, use the ALT key with the down arrow.

On a 160K disk, you will be able to store 1100 forms. On the 320K disk, you will be able to store 2200 forms.

Trademarks

The italicized names are trademarked products of the corresponding companies, with registered trademarks noted with an ® and service marks noted with an ^SM.

1-2-3	Lotus Development Corporation
APIO	Transend Corporation
Apple ®	Apple Computer, Inc.
ASIO	Transend Corporation
Axiom	Axiom Corporation
Bizcomp ®	Bizcomp Corporation
Chameleon ®	Sperry Univac
COMPAQ	COMPAQ Computer Corporation
CompuServe ®	CompuServe, Inc.
Corona PC	Corona Data Systems
dBASE II ®	Ashton-Tate
DIALOG ®	DIALOG Information Services, Inc.
Dot Plot	Dataproducts Corporation
Dow Jones News/Retrieval ®	Dow Jones and Company
Eagle ®	Eagle Computers
EasyLink ^SM	Western Union Telegraph Company
Epson	Epson America, Inc.
Framework	Ashton-Tate
FX-80	Epson America, Inc.
Graphitti	Prometheus Products
Graphtrax ®	Epson America, Inc.
Grappler, Grappler + ®	Orange Micro, Inc.
Hayes ®	Hayes Microcomputer Products, Inc.
HP	Hewlett-Packard
Hyperion ®	Bytec-Comterm, Inc.
IBM ®	International Business Machines, Inc.
KNOWLEDGE INDEX ^SM	DIALOG Information Services, Inc.
KnowledgeMan	Micro Data Base Systems, Inc.
Lotus	Lotus Development Corporation
Macintosh	Apple Computer, Inc.

Mailgram ®	Western Union Telegraph Company
MCI Mail	MCI Communications Corporation
MPI ®	Micro Peripherals, Inc.
MS ®	Microsoft Corporation
Multi-Personal Computer	Columbia Data Products
Multiplan	Microsoft Corporation
MX-70	Epson America, Inc.
MX-80	Epson America, Inc.
MX-100	Epson America, Inc.
NEC	NEC Information Systems
Novation ®	Novation, Inc.
Okidata	Okidata
Okigraph	Okidata
Password	U.S. Robotics, Inc.
PC: IntelliModem	Bizcomp Corporation
PC ModemCard	Transend Corporation
PC Modem Plus ®	Ven - Tel
PFS: ®	Software Publishing Company
POPCOM X100	Prentice Corporation
Profile	Apple Computer, Inc.
Selectric	International Business Machines, Inc.
Silentype ®	Apple Computer, Inc.
Smartcom	Hayes Microcomputer Products, Inc.
SmartModem	Hayes Microcomputer Products, Inc.
Strobe	Strobe, Inc.
Sweet-p ®	Enter Computer, Inc.
Symphony	Lotus Development Corporation
Telenet	Telenet Communications Corporation
The Source SM	The Source Telecomputing Corporation
TI ®	Texas Instruments, Inc.
TI Professional	Texas Instruments, Inc.
Transend ®	Transend Corporation
UPI	United Press International
U.S. Robotics ®	U.S. Robotics
Ven - Tel ®	Ven - Tel
Versacard	Prometheus Products
VisiCalc ®	VisiCorp
WordStar ®	MicroPro International

Index